Preaching as Dialogue

Is the Sermon a Sacred Cow?

Jeremy Thomson

Lecturer in Religious Studies, Birkbeck College and
Tutor on the Oasis Youth Work and Ministry Course, London

GROVE BOOKS LIMITED
RIDLEY HALL RD CAMBRIDGE CB3 9HU

Contents

The Cover Illustration is by Peter Ashton

First Impression December 1996
Second Edition March 2003
ISSN 0144-171X
ISBN 1 85174 332 4

Introduction

1

For centuries preaching has been integral to church life. Many ministers believe that the preparation and delivery of sermons is one of their most important tasks (if not the most important).

Christians think of hearing God's word as they read the Bible, and perhaps in other ways—but there is something special about preaching. Preaching appears to offer an opportunity of hearing God's word for a specific situation through someone whom God has particularly gifted for the task. It is more than teaching individuals (though that may be one result), it is what one particular gathering of Christians needs to hear—vision, encouragement, consolation, challenge, correction, warning. Yet as I have listened to sermons and preached them myself, I have become uneasy about the exalted place the sermon enjoys in Christian estimation.

For all the effort of preparing, delivering and listening to sermons, most church members are not as mature as we might expect as a result. Why is this? Of course, there are bad sermons, and there are preachers whose lives are inconsistent with their teaching. But people may listen week by week to the best prepared and presented sermons, given by thoroughly sincere preachers, and yet make little progress in Christian discipleship. Some preachers blame congregations for a lack of expectancy that God will speak, for an inability to listen to a 'solid exposition,' or even for disobedience to what they hear. But I suspect that there is a more significant factor in the failure rate of the sermon than the quality of the preacher or the responsiveness of the hearers.

I have become uneasy about the exalted place the sermon enjoys in Christian expectation

I want to suggest that the problem lies in our concept of preaching itself; preaching has become stereotyped into sermons. To explain what I mean by this distinction between preaching and sermons, I suggest that we consider the activity of preaching (and its reception) as *a social phenomenon*, that is, let us examine the *setting* and *format* of the interaction between the participants. I shall show below that preaching in the New Testament exhibits a great variety of settings and formats. In contrast, virtually all contemporary sermons have certain stereotyped social features, however they may vary in terms of content, theology, aim, length, style or delivery. They are delivered in the context of a service of worship, often from a pulpit, and they are almost entirely monologues. The only exception is to be found in those Pentecostal churches where the congregation interjects responses to the preacher. But even these responses make very little difference to the essentially monologue format of the sermon. In social terms nearly all of us think of a sermon in terms of an appointed preacher speaking from a symbolic location to a congregation which does not interact verbally with the preacher.

Preaching has become stereotyped into sermons

There are a number of advocates of the sermon who have responded to the criticism of its alleged ineffectiveness.[1] While much that they write is valuable, they do not consider the sermon as a social phenomenon. They find the *raison d'être* of the sermon in the preaching to which the Bible alludes, and in its historical development. Some emphasize the importance of the listener, advocating the ideal of a dialogue (albeit unspoken) between preacher and congregation. But they maintain that even if communication or educational studies raise questions about the effectiveness of sermons, the theological undergirding of sermons remains and justifies them. Thus they implicitly advocate the retention of the stereotyped setting and format of the sermon.

In this booklet I will examine preaching in the New Testament as a social phenomenon, and then provide a brief account of the historical development of the sermon. I will go on to outline the theology of preaching in the Reformation and in this century to explore how the sermon acquired its exalted status. Next, the criticisms I make of the theology of the sermon require me to develop a theology of preaching as a dialogue. Finally, I discuss the practical implications of the argument by setting out some principles for preaching and by analysing actual attempts to put them into practice.

Preaching in the New Testament as a Social Phenomenon   2

One of the more difficult areas of biblical interpretation is that of handling a term, the meaning of which has subtly changed over the years.

Awareness of cultural changes is necessary in order to avoid mistaken application to the contemporary world. It is vital that we grasp this point: *there is a real difference between the usual understanding of preaching today—the sermon—and preaching in the Bible.*

The Old Testament provides important background for our understanding of preaching, but here I shall concentrate on the New Testament texts. Of obvious significance are the terms *kerysso* (to proclaim), *angello* (to announce), *euangelizomai* (to bring good news), and their compounds and cognates. The activity that these words convey is generally one of open and public proclamation of God's word and acts. But, as we shall see, any consideration of preaching must take into account many other related expressions, particularly those associated with prophecy (*propheteuo*, to prophecy), and with teaching, (*katecheo*, to instruct; *didasko*, to teach). The distinction which C H Dodd made between *kerygma* and *didache* (preaching and teaching) has been influential, but it cannot be maintained at the level of terminology.[2] However, consideration of the audience clearly affected the content of Paul's speaking (compare his address in the synagogue at Antioch, Acts 13.13-48, with that to Athenians, Acts 17.22-34), and his letters to churches are geared primarily to their need of teaching rather than to preaching to unbelievers. Jesus, on at least some occasions, made a clear distinction between the way he taught his disciples and the way he taught others (see, for instance, Mk 4.10-12). Thus social setting must be as important a consideration as terminology in our examination of the texts.

Social setting must be as important a consideration as terminology in our examination of the texts

The first three Gospels portray Jesus preaching or teaching in the synagogue and the temple, but also in other settings (here I will confine references to

Mark): addressing crowds from the door of a home (Mk 2.2; cf 3.19-35), at the meal table (Mk 2.15-17; 14.3-9), by the sea or from a boat (Mk 2.13; 3.9; 4.1), going through fields (Mk 2.23) and in a remote place (Mk 6.34). Jesus teaches the disciples privately on the road (Mk 8.27-31; 10.17-31, 32-45), in houses (Mk 7.17-23; 9.33; 10.10) and while sightseeing on the Mount of Olives (Mk 13). As to format, much of Jesus' teaching was remembered and written down in short, pithy sayings (often using poetry, riddles or questions), or parables.[3] In addition there are a few extended discourses delivered to a 'passive' audience (for example in Mk 4.1ff; 6.34; 13.3ff).[4]

Much of Jesus' teaching was given 'on the way' and involved a high degree of interaction with the audience

Much of Jesus' teaching was given 'on the way' and involved a high degree of interaction with the audience (Mk 8.27-10.52). There were many occasions when it arose out of a question or an incident (Mk 2.18-28; 7.1-23; 9.33-37, and even 13.3ff), and it frequently included interaction with his hearers (Mk 8.14-21; 10.23-31, 35-45). The culmination of Jesus' preaching in the Synoptic Gospels took place in the temple, where he was constantly responding to aggressive questions (Mk 11.27-12.44). Finally, it is important to consider the teaching impact of many of Jesus' actions. As well as some clearly symbolic or figurative activity (Mk 3.14-19; 11.12-14 & 20-25), much of what Jesus did conveyed an emphatic message (Mk 2.15-17).

In John's Gospel we find Jesus sitting by a well, preaching by means of an extended conversation (4.7-26), a format which he had also employed with Nicodemus (3.1-15). Having invited suggestions from the disciples about how to feed the large crowd, the next day Jesus provokes questions amongst the crowd, Jewish critics and his disciples about bread from heaven (6.1-69). In the temple Jesus teaches the crowds and interacts with critics on several occasions (7.14-52; 8.12-59; 10.1-39). The man born blind testifies to Jesus as prophet and healer in an altercation with the Pharisees and finally comes to believe in the Son of Man when he has a conversation with him (9.1-41). The so-called upper-room discourse includes extensive interaction with the disciples (14.1-16.33).[5]

In the book of Acts we find that the apostles preached in the temple and synagogue (eg Acts 4.2; 13.5), but also in Cornelius' house (Acts 10.24-44), to a few women by the riverside (Acts 16.13), in prison (Acts 16.31), and in the hall of Tyrannus in Ephesus (Acts 19.9). Philip preached the good news to one man in his chariot (Acts 8.35). We tend to think of Paul preaching in the form of a speech, as in the synagogue at Antioch (Acts 13.16-41) or in front of the Areopagus (Acts 17.22-31), but we should note that the speech in Athens came at the invitation of those who had heard Paul arguing in the market place (Acts 17.17-19). In fact his preaching more often took the form of argument, explanation and persuasion, as Luke records in Thessalonica, Corinth, Ephesus, in prison in Caesarea, and at Rome (Acts 17.2; 18.4, 19; 19.8f; 24.25f; 28.23f). In a rare article in this area, Stanley Stowers examines the circumstances of Paul's preaching activity and shows that the most significant settings for it were the private house and the leather workshop. He concludes that 'the widespread picture of Paul the public orator, sophist or street corner preacher is a false one.'[6]

So, when Paul wrote things like 'how are they to hear without someone to proclaim him' (Rom 10.14), or 'Woe to me if I do not proclaim the gospel!' (1 Cor 9.16), he was not thinking primarily of giving a sermon from a pulpit (as do most preachers today), but of taking any opportunity to explain the gospel and to convince whomever he met. He could adapt his preaching format to suit the social setting, and this often meant that he used an interactive means of presenting the gospel.

Paul could adapt his preaching format to suit the social setting

As well as preaching to unbelievers, teaching the churches was often informal and interactive. At Troas Paul spoke to the believers through the night (Acts 20.7-12), but we should not think of this as a monologue (as some translators erroneously imply: the RSV has 'speech' at v 7b), interrupted only by Eutychus' fall from the window; the use of *dialegomai* (discussion) in vv 7 and 9 indicates verbal interaction between Paul and his hearers.[7] After Eutychus' recovery and a meal, Paul continued his conversation (*homileo*, cf Lk 24.14, 15; Acts 20.11; 24.26) until dawn in v11. Another format which the apostolic teaching took was that of writing. Some letters were very much part of an ongoing interaction (especially the Corinthian and Thessalonian correspondence). It must not be forgotten that the message of the apostles (like that of Jesus) was embodied in the way they lived as much as in what they said (for example 'So deeply do we care for you that we are determined to share with you not only the gospel of God but also our own selves, because you have become very dear to us.' 1 Thess 2.8; see also 2 Cor 4.7-12).

Some had a gift for teaching but teaching was also a mutual responsibility of all

Some had a particular gift for teaching in the early church (Rom 12.7; 1 Cor 12.28; Eph 4.11; 1 Tim 5.17; 2 Tim 2.2). Yet teaching was also a mutual responsibility of all: 'teach and admonish one another in all wisdom' (Col 3.16); 'you yourselves are full of goodness, filled with all knowledge, and able to instruct one another' (Rom 15.14; see also 1 Thess 5.11, 14). This reciprocal pronoun 'one another' (*allelon*) is an important part of early Christian ecclesiology, occurring 23 times in the epistles in sections of admonition (*paraklesis*).[8] The few details that we have of the meetings of Christians suggest a much greater degree of contribution and interaction among the participants than we are used to in conventional services of worship (see 1 Cor 14.26; Eph 5.19).[9] To advance the gospel the believers in general were exhorted to engage in worthwhile conversations with outsiders (Col 4.5f; 1 Pet 3.15).

We may conclude the following about preaching or teaching as a social phenomenon in the New Testament:

i) It was not confined to a formal or religious setting, but often took place in homes, outdoors and on the road.

ii) As much as a planned or regular activity, preaching arose spontaneously as Jesus and the early Christians involved themselves with the lives of others. It entailed recognizing and challenging assumptions, and dealing with questions raised by others.

iii) Preaching was not confined to any particular size of group, but was addressed to individuals, families and small groups as much as to larger gatherings.

iv) Only sometimes did preaching take the format of a monologue. There were speeches, but these were frequently given in the context of discussion, and they often included interaction with the audience. Argument and discussion were important means of persuasive preaching.

v) Preaching was not confined to the spoken word. It could take the form of writing, and was as much a matter of behaviour as of words.

From Preaching to Sermons 3

Nigel Watson is one of few recent writers to make explicit the fact that,

> Preaching has evolved over the centuries and only by degrees attained a clearly defined form. That form results from the confluence over some generations of several lines of tradition...This means that, as normally practised today, preaching does not correspond exactly to any one of the various ministries of the word about which we read in the New Testament but has elements of them all.[10]

The earliest available evidence that we have of preaching after the New Testament period indicates that it took the form of a simple practical and pastoral 'homily' (from the Latin '*homilio*,' conversation) based on a text, often delivered extempore and without rhetorical structure. It has been suggested that this was influenced by patterns of synagogue worship, in which a reading from Scripture was followed by an explanation of a passage.[11] Several interlinking historical factors can be proposed in the development of the stereotyped sermon. The sheer size of developing Christian gatherings made interaction between preacher and congregation more problematic. Churches developed a liturgical style of worship which required a more formal ministry of the word, which in turn encouraged the appropriation of traditional rhetorical techniques by third and fourth century preachers. The proliferation of heresy focused attention on the teaching of recognized church leaders; a special priestly role and authority came to be attributed to them and a clergy-laity divide developed.

However, a number of patristic writings reflect a dialogical means of communicating the gospel. Justin Martyr's *Dialogue with Trypho* (160-165 AD) portrays a private conversation in the midst of friends, and in fact places one dialogue within another dialogue. Tertullian's *Against the Jews* (before 200 AD) is cast as a debate between a Christian and a Jewish proselyte. In Origen's *Against Celsus* (250 AD) the argument takes the form of a debate with some Jewish 'wise men.' Theophilus' *To Autolycus* is an elaboration of a discussion with a distinguished pagan.[12] Of course, it is difficult to know how much dialogue as a literary device reflects dialogue in the flesh, but there does seem evidence here of a dialogical approach to communicating the gospel, at least to outsiders.

In the Middle Ages, the friars and Lollards revived peripatetic preaching, and more interactive teaching occurred in dissenting groups where Scripture was translated into the vernacular such as the Waldensian cells. Preaching was vital to the Reformers, yet the renewed awareness of the 'priesthood of all believers' did little to break down the division between the ordained minister or clergyman and the laity, and preaching largely retained its stereotyped setting and format. Nonconformist preachers in England operated in a variety of settings and placed emphasis on small groups with greater participation (especially John Wesley). In contemporary church life small groups are significant, though not all of them have a strong learning element, and preaching is still generally thought of in terms of the stereotyped sermon. Martin Lloyd-Jones, the revered minister of Westminster Chapel, said of monologue preaching: 'it is God's own method.'[13]

4

The Theology of Preaching Sermons

a) The Reformers

Preaching the Word of God was central to the Reformation. Martin Luther's rediscovery of justification by grace through faith meant that this Pauline doctrine had to be declared. Thus the sermon had to become the very centre of the service of worship. Preaching was a dynamic or even an apocalyptic event in which a battle for souls was fought with the adversary, and Jesus Christ came to the hearer with his salvation. Klaas Runia introduces a quotation from Luther thus: 'But above all it was a *saving* event. In the preaching of the gospel Jesus Christ himself comes to us with all his salvation.'[14]

> God the Creator of heaven and earth, speaks with you through his preachers, baptizes, catechizes, absolves you through the ministry of his own sacraments. These are the words of God, not of Plato or Aristotle. It is God Himself who speaks.[15]

For Luther, preaching performs its supreme function at the crisis of salvation. This view is reinforced by the almost numinous quality that the preacher acquires with respect to the hearer. Of course, Luther's vast output of sermons demonstrates that his was no narrow gospel; he could take for a theme the sublimity of God or the greed of a sow. It was the task of the minister to expound the Scriptures since only they expose human sinfulness and bring healing for life's hurts.[16]

For John Calvin also the preacher was 'the mouth of God,'[17] but with a more clearly defined responsibility to build up the church; preaching took priority over discipline as a means of social change. In the *Institutes* Calvin quotes Eph 4.10-13; Christ 'appointed some to be apostles, some prophets, some evangelists, some pastors and teachers, for the equipment of the saints, for the work of ministry, for the building up of the body of Christ, until we all reach the unity of faith and of the knowledge of the Son of God, to perfect manhood, to the measure of the fully mature age of Christ.' He goes on to say,

> We see how God, who could in a moment perfect his own, nevertheless desires them to grow up into manhood solely under the education of the church. We see the way set for it: the preaching of the heavenly doctrine has been enjoined upon the pastors. We see that all are brought under the same regulation, that with a gentle and teachable spirit they may allow themselves to be governed by teachers appointed to this function.[18]

Calvin believed that congregations had a real responsibility as listeners to preaching, but in social terms they should be passive receptors of sermons. Here he elevates the authority of the preacher using the terms 'regulation' and 'government,' implying congregational acquiescence so that any format other than the monologue sermon is unthinkable. As John Leith says, preaching has become a 'sacrament of the saving presence of God…something of a divine epiphany.'[19]

However, I must point out that something different is implied in the verses which follow the quoted passage in Eph 4; 'But speaking the truth (*aletheuo*) in love, we must grow up in every way into him who is the head, into Christ.' (v15, cf Gal 4.16)[20] The vision of the church here is not one of an asymmetric relationship between gifted leaders and a docile flock, but one of maturity for all, achieved by a process of truthful and loving interchange, facilitated by gifted people.

Calvin proceeds to rely heavily upon Old Testament references to priests and prophets to bolster the authority of the preacher, laying stress on the formal, religious setting of the Temple.

> [God] willed of old that holy assemblies be held at the sanctuary in order that the doctrine taught by the mouth of the priest might foster agreement in faith, The Temple is called God's 'resting place' (Ps 32.14);

> the sanctuary, his 'dwelling' (Isa 57.15), where he is said to sit among the cherubim (Ps 80.1). Glorious titles, they are used solely to bring esteem, love, reverence, and dignity to the ministry of the heavenly doctrine.[21]

He goes on to make the extraordinary claim 'that the church is built up solely by outward preaching' and indicates that buildings become sacred through preaching: 'By his Word, God alone sanctifies temples to himself for lawful use.' In espousing the formal religious setting, Calvin makes no distinction between the Old Testament people of God and the New Testament understanding of the church in his discourse on preaching. Yet it seems to me that the pouring out of the Spirit on the church marks a significant discontinuity and introduces a significant element of mutuality into the preacher-congregation relationship, as we shall see below.

An accurate summary of the Reformers' understanding of preaching is given by T H L Parker: they 'all interpreted the power of the keys as the church's preaching...because the gospel preached is God's word, this is the verdict of God himself, so to say, his judgment seat the pulpit.'[22]

b) This Century

In the first part of the *Church Dogmatics* (1/1, 56), Karl Barth demonstrated his continuity with the Reformers in his quotation from the Second Helvetic Confession: *Praedicatio verbi Dei est verbum Dei* (The preaching of the word of God is the word of God).[23] For him preaching is one of three forms of God's Word along with the written Word and the Living Word.

> The language about God to be found in the church is meant to be proclamation, so far as it is directed towards man in the form of preaching and sacrament, with the claim and in an atmosphere of expectation that in accordance with its mission it has to tell him the Word of God to be heard in faith.[24]

Barth's adoption of the term 'proclamation' gave the preacher the same aura of unquestionability that it had for the Reformers.

While there are similarities between the Reformers' view of preaching and that of Barth, his is significantly different in that it is controlled by his actualist concept of revelation. The initiative is always with God and, just as the Bible cannot be equated with God's Word, but must *become* the Word of God, so also preaching must *become* the Word of God.[25] All that the preacher is required to do is to repeat in his own words the biblical witness to Jesus Christ as the revealing and reconciling Word of God, and the reception of the message by the listeners may be safely left to God.[26]

Barth does at times acknowledge that the preacher should bear the life-situation of the listener in mind, but what really concerned him was a person's situation before God.

> A preacher is called to lead to God the people whom he sees before him; God desires him to preach to these people here present. But he must approach them as people who are already the object of God's action, for whom Christ died and has risen again. He has to tell them, therefore, that God's mercy avails for them as truly today as at the beginning of time. That is what is meant by adapting preaching to the congregation.[27]

Although many were initially encouraged by Barth's view of preaching, a reaction set in against it because it gave insufficient consideration to the life of the listeners in their own particular historical situation.[28] It was recognized that, at least at the level of homiletics, issues of communication must be addressed by the preacher.

One of the most elevated contemporary expressions of the high view of sermons which I have found is that of James Daane, a founding editor of *The Reformed Journal*. His book, *Preaching With Confidence*, was written in 1980 in reaction to calls for the communication of biblical truth through Christian action; its subtitle is 'A theological essay on the power of the pulpit.'

> The Bible is indeed the written form of the Word of God. But the Word finds a higher expression in that personal form of it which takes place in the pulpit of the church, for the pulpit expression which is true to the written Word approximates more closely that Word which became flesh in Jesus Christ, because it is itself an expression of that fleshly, human form in which the Word of God is present in Jesus Christ.[29]

Now, many people could testify that God has spoken to them through the words and life of someone they know, although they had previously been impervious to any reading of the Bible. It is to be hoped that there will be a correlation between the Word made flesh in Jesus Christ and the ministry of one of his disciples (though I would not describe this as 'a higher expression' of God's Word than that in the Bible). But Daane's application of this correlation to preaching in the pulpit would only make sense if the incarnation took place entirely within a pulpit! He has made the mistake of assuming that a pulpit sermon is equivalent to the preaching found in the Bible.

Few who hold a high theology of the sermon give theological reasons for rejecting some form of dialogue with the recipients of preaching. But Martin Lloyd-Jones refused any idea of dialogue in the proclamation of the gospel on the theological grounds that,

God is not to be discussed or debated. God is not a subject for debate, because He is Who He is and What He is. We are told that the unbeliever, of course, does not agree with that; and that is perfectly true; but that makes no difference. We believe it, and it is part of our very case to assert it. Holding the view that we do, believing what we do about God, we cannot in any circumstances allow Him to become a subject for discussion or of debate or investigation. I base my argument at this point on the word addressed by God Himself to Moses at the burning bush (Exod 3.1-6). Moses had suddenly seen this remarkable phenomenon of the burning bush, and was proposing to turn aside and to examine this astonishing phenomenon. But immediately he is rebuked by the voice...That seems to me to be the governing principle in this whole matter.[30]

There is here a proper concern for the seriousness of the subject, but God's holiness does not prohibit a dialogical communication between God and human beings. To take Lloyd-Jones' own example: immediately following God's self announcement and commissioning at the burning bush, Moses responds with several reservations and questions, each of which is answered by God (Exod 3.11- 4.17). The dialogue is actually concerned with more than simple clarification of communication, it is about Moses' reluctance and inadequacy (or even, initially, his legitimate needs) in order to fulfil God's call and God's willingness to negotiate about them. This is one of the wonders of God's self-revelation to human beings: God takes human personality utterly seriously, graciously allows questions and supplies answers in a dialogical relationship. This quintessential account of God's call of Moses, reflected in many parts of the Old Testament, impels us to reject a monological theology of the sermon.

A Theology of Preaching as a Dialogue

5

I have just asserted that it is in God's own nature to engage in dialogue with human beings.

Of course, there are occasions where God speaks without engaging in dialogue with human beings (eg Gen 1.28-30). Even Moses, who managed to change God's mind through dialogue on several occasions, received a rebuff over his desire to cross the Jordan (Deut 3.23-27). On the eve of Israel's destruction and exile, the prophets conveyed God's withdrawal from dialogue (Jer 7.16). Jesus' devastating criticism of the pharisees (Matt 23) concludes with an announcement of Jerusalem's destruction which allows no debate. Even so, there may be times when a preacher has to convey a message which allows for no disputation. However, these situations are not the norm between God and his people. Abraham (Gen 18.16-33), Joshua (Josh 5.13-15), Samuel (1 Sam 8.4-22), Elijah (1 Kings 19.9-18) and other prophets have conversations with God, and if it should be objected that these were leaders in Israel, then I would argue that preachers should have Moses' desire for all God's people to be touched by God's Spirit (Num 11.29)—in fact, more than a desire, a recognition that this has occurred, because we must read the Old Testament in the light of Christ and of the coming of the Spirit at Pentecost.

Preachers should have Moses' desire for all God's people to be touched by God's Spirit

Next, I want to argue for a relational, dialogical understanding of the image of God in human beings, such as has been developed by Alistair McFadyen in *The Call to Personhood*. In the vertical dimension, human beings are called and invited into a dialogical relationship with God rather than subjected to megaphone-style address and manipulating power. The creative and sustaining activity of God is intended to call forth a grateful human response, as seen particularly in the psalms of thanksgiving and praise. In the horizontal dimension, the creation of human beings in the image of the triune God (understood socially), yields a relational understanding of people embodied in the male-female encounter. People gradually acquire competence in the communicative procedures of a linguistic community and thereby develop a subjectivity which is inherently relational rather than self-constituting. However, in the fallen world, social processes are frequently distorted so that some persons with access to power deny the personhood of those with less power. As a result, these weaker ones experience the constraints of an imposed identity. The result is distorted communication. McFadyen identifies distorted communication with monologue and genuine communication with dialogue.[31]

McFadyen extends the relational understanding of personhood into the doctrine of redemption by considering the call to discipleship. Jesus' call to the first disciples appears as an abrupt command, requiring them to move out of their formative social networks. It cannot be accounted for on human grounds; it is a recreative call introducing revolutionary possibilities. This call does not negate the personhood of the disciples; it transforms their previous identity by a new orientation of obedience and service, based in an open fellowship directed towards God and others.[32] I would add that we have seen that the relationship between Jesus and his disciples is dialogical. The initiative, the example, the authoritative teaching come from Jesus, but the disciples are encouraged to respond with questions, expressions of puzzlement and contributions of their own (for example Peter's observation of the withered fig tree and interpretation of Jesus' word to it as a curse; Mk 11.12-14, 20-22). In some ways, the most astonishing incident in the gospels is the encounter of Jesus with the Syrophoenician woman who 'knows who Jesus is and holds him to it.'[33]

Francis Watson employs McFadyen's understanding of communication in a theological interpretation of Paul's teaching on spiritual gifts in 1 Cor 14:

> *if the movement from distorted, monological communication to undistorted, dialogical communication is interpreted by the church as both redemptive and anticipatory of the eschatological future of the kingdom of God, then this process of interpretation must itself be dialogical...*If the image of God in the other constitutes a call to dialogue—rather than, say, a monologue addressed by either party to the other, or mutual indifference—then the same will be true when God's presence in the other is mediated not only in the universal form of the image of God but in the concrete form of the Word of God. We will, in fact, have to relativize the idea that human utterance of the word of God is an *office* held on a permanent basis by certain individual members of the community—apostles, prophets, ministers, priests, bishops—whose role is to transmit a word which must simply be acknowledged by the rest of the community. Such a view is fundamentally monological (or logocentric). While particular office-holders can be the initiators of communication, it is more appropriate to see the revelation or word of God as located within the process of dialogue thereby initiated than to locate it solely in the statement that opens it.[34]

If the Holy Spirit inspires the prophet, then it is implied that the same Spirit is at work in the process of judging what is said (1 Cor 14.29). That process may require interaction for the purposes of clarification, interpretation, and application (as when Paul implicitly refuses to act on Agabus' prophetic warning in Acts 21.10-14). Watson points out that the readers of the *Didache* were instructed not to 'test or examine any prophet speaking in the Spirit, for every sin shall be forgiven, but this sin shall not be forgiven' (11.7)[35] Perhaps we can see here early signs of a trend which came to locate the manifestation of the Spirit in the specially ordained man rather than in the whole congregation, and thus to move preaching towards the authoritarian monologue.

The underlying issue here is whether the Spirit is present and at work in the Christian community as a whole, rather than focused solely in the one gifted speaker. I have found Robert Banks' work on *Paul's Idea of Community* illuminating here. He sees Paul's understanding of fellowship in the church in contrast with Jewish religious associations where 'participation in the fraternity centred primarily around a *code*, as embodied in the Torah,' and in another contrast with Hellenistic religious associations where 'participation in the fraternity centred primarily around a *cult*.'

According to Paul's understanding, participation in the community centred primarily around *fellowship*, expressed in word and deed, of the members with God and one another...This means that the focal point of reference was neither a book nor a rite but *a set of relationships*, and that God communicated himself to them not primarily through the written word and tradition, or mystical experience and cultic activity, but *through one another*. Certainly fellowship is not altogether lacking in these other groups, ranging as they do from the comparative individualism of the mysteries to the strong community at Qumran, nor are the Old Testament scriptures and various corporate activities absent from the Pauline churches. But a real difference lies at the heart of their respective gatherings. This makes it impossible for Paul's approach as to what happens in church to have been derived in any fundamental way from the practice of the synagogue or of the cults. For him something quite new has broken into human experience, and this is nothing less than the 'first fruits' or anticipation of that community between God and his people that will be ushered in at the Last Day.[36]

It is this understanding of the communication of God's own self through one another which realizes the doctrine of the indwelling of the Spirit in the whole community.[37] Once this is acknowledged, preaching within the church must be understood as facilitating the growth to maturity of all through the communication of God's Word, rather than as channelling God's Word to the people through a single proclaimer.

Beginning in the 1970s various theologians have sought to apply the category of narrative to theological problems, and to communicating theology to church members. James McClendon and Stanley Hauerwas sought to draw out the link between story and life, arguing that ethics comes at the beginning of Christian theological reflection. The central ethical question is 'What constitutes a good person?' rather than 'What constitutes a good action?' In turn, the 'good person' is related to the Christian community since that is the focal point of the development of a people of character.[38] Now one of the central features of narrative and of community is dialogue; without verbal interaction characters in a narrative can have only a limited development. Likewise there must be a dialogue between teachers and learners if there is to be maturity in the church community; how can characters develop without the opportunity to verbalize? How can a community be a community if one person does all the talking? This is not to deny that some characters within a narrative or a community have authority with respect to others, or a message to pass on to them. But if preaching is to take seriously the wealth and nature of dialogue within the biblical narrative, it must incorporate explicit dialogue.

More recently Ched Myers has followed up his important political reading of Mark's Gospel with a passionate exercise in what he calls 'interrogatory theology' (building on McClendon).

> More than three-quarters of the episodes in [Mark's] gospel are composed around questions to, by or about Jesus—from his inaugural challenge to scribal authority (1.24) to the story's closing quandary (16.3). Jesus is presented not as a sage who explains life's mysteries but as the great interlocutor of reality. His queries lay bare the 'inner conflicts' of disciples and opponents alike (Gk *dialogizesthai*; 2.8; 8.16f; 9.33f; 11.31). Sometimes they are sharply rhetorical: 'Can Satan exorcize Satan?' (3.23); 'What will the owner of the vineyard do?' (12.9). Other times they are wrapped in metaphor or parable: 'is a lamp brought indoors to be put under a basket?' (4.21); 'Should wedding guests fast while the bridegroom is with them?' (2.19). But always they challenge both the ideology of the dominant culture ('How can the scribes say...?' 12.35) and the theology of disciples ('Do you not yet understand?' 8.21). Above all, they call into question our biblical literacy: 'Have you never read...?' (2.25; 12.10); 'Is it not written...?' (9.12; 11.17).[39]

The greatest preacher of them all asked questions, brought people into the conversation, took the observations and questions of others as opportunities to tackle the burning issues of life. Why have preachers forsaken him in this?

Finally, two remarks about our notions of authority which may lie at the heart of our problems with monologue preaching.

Firstly, Jurgen Moltmann has argued that the Christian church has been unduly influenced by a hierarchical view of reality which goes hand-in-hand with an overemphasis on monotheism to the neglect of the Trinity understood in social terms (three persons united in perfect love).

> The doctrine of the Trinity which evolves out of the surmounting of monotheism for Christ's sake, must therefore overcome this monarchism, which legitimates dependency, helplessness and servitude.[40]

To be critical of hierarchy is not to deny that there is a place for leadership, structure or even institution. But all these must be concerned with and practised in the service of the whole church rather than as a means to power for certain individuals. There is a great asymmetry of power between the monologue preacher and the passive congregation.

Secondly, Jesus practised and taught what I call 'lowerarchy': 'You know that among the Gentiles those whom they recognize as their rulers lord it over them, and their great ones are tyrants over them. But it is not so among you: whoever wishes to become great among you must be your servant, and whoever wishes to be first among you must be slave of all.' (Mk 10.42-44) This subversion of the normal understanding of authority is characteristic of Jesus' whole project. Ian McFarland comments on Jesus' response to Peter's confession at Caesarea Philippi (Matt 16.21-23),

> Far from being beyond question, Jesus' authority as the Christ is here associated directly with the fate of being held up to question and rejected. This episode thus provides a bridgehead to the idea that being held accountable may not compromise authority, but actually enhance it…it is necessary to look beyond the fact *that* God identifies with the community in Jesus to an examination of *how* God does so. As the Gospels describe it, such identification is not effected from the top down, but, so to speak, 'from the outside in.' In other words, Jesus does not simply minister to those at the margins of the covenant community, but actually claims his authority from there.[41]

The church must be careful to follow its founder in its use of power, and ensure that its preaching is not 'six feet above contradiction.'

There is a link between Moltmann's social doctrine of the Trinity, McFadyen's social understanding of personhood and my social analysis of preaching in the New Testament. It seems to me that theology must pay greater attention to the social dimension of reality, especially if it is going to fulfil one of its main tasks, that of reforming the life of the church. The case for preaching dialogically is a matter of effective communication, but it so because this is part of a profound theological understanding of life's social dimension.

Practical Implications   6

If the church is to take seriously the Bible's own models for preaching and if the theological argument for a dialogical practice of preaching has been established, then:

(i) It must be recognized that informal conversations or group activities dealing with the gospel and the Christian life are as much preaching as any church sermon. As David Buttrick says in his huge book *Homiletic*: 'The notion that the laity is assigned a work of preaching the gospel, though unexceptional, is seldom taken seriously.'[42]

(ii) While teaching activities are vital to the life of the church, it must be recognized that all aspects of church life convey messages to members and non-members, and they should be consciously reviewed in this light.

(iii) The conventional sermon can no longer be regarded as the preaching format. Changes must be introduced to allow preaching to be explicitly dialogical.

I want to concentrate on (iii), which has the most controversial implications. I will set out some principles, explore some possibilities and counter one or two objections.

a) Some Principles

1. We Must Repent of the Sacred Cow of the Sermon

I mean that we must allow the biblical examples of Jesus and of Paul to question the engrained assumption that to preach sermons is to fulfil the responsibility to preach and teach. We need to reassess the aims and methods that our churches have adopted (seldom explicitly) in order to communicate the faith, and to understand them in the light of the wider command to make disciples. This may mean that a conventional sermon may be the most effective means of preaching from time to time; I do not mean that we must abandon the sermon altogether.

2. We Must Reassess the Goal of our Preaching in Terms of Setting

Some preachers of sermons place so much emphasis upon the gospel (in fact I would describe theirs as a narrow understanding of the gospel), that their churches receive little teaching geared to discipleship. In the social setting of a church gathering, in which most of the liturgical assumptions are that the participants are willing to assent to Christian faith, preaching should largely aim at teaching believers. It is true that responsible and effective preaching of the gospel, geared to unbelievers, will contain elements of teaching which may edify those who are already Christians. However, consideration of the social setting of preaching should inform the goal of preaching. If the intention is to bring people to Christian faith for the first time, then preaching must take place in a social setting where such people are to be found, or into which they can be invited and made to feel comfortable. Such settings will probably be outside church buildings altogether. I do not deny that there are plenty of nominal Christians within church buildings, but a challenge to live out their Christian confession would seem nearer to Paul's dealings with such people.

3. We Must Reassess the Methods of our Preaching in Terms of Format

We should take seriously the communicative and educative dimensions of preaching, as exemplified in the Bible. Theories of communication and education may provide insight for preachers, but for Christians the scriptural models of communication and education should count most because they embody the normative Christian attitudes to inter-human relationships and to the development of human maturity.[43] In particular, preachers should move away from the exclusively monologue format, and find ways to encourage interactive involvement of congregations.

4. The Role of the Preacher Must be Balanced with the Role of the Recipient

In advocating interactive learning, I want to guard against the pooling of ignorance. Discussion amongst novices without some element of oversight and teaching input will come to grief. Yet it is also possible for someone to give a presentable monologue without knowing much about the subject, so the traditional sermon does not protect the congregation from this problem. I would maintain that the true knowledge and skill of a teacher emerges in interaction with learners. Certain people demonstrate the ability to help others to a greater understanding and more consistent lifestyle. They speak, they ask questions and provoke questions; they set some people tasks and involve others in projects, enabling reflection on these activities. They know when to step back and encourage group discussion, and when to intervene in order to maintain the aims of the activity. They know that they themselves are not the fount of all wisdom and knowledge, and are pleased to discover others who can make a worthwhile contribution. They train others to take over their role.

The recipient of effective preaching and teaching is one whose thinking and behaviour moves on in living response to God's word. A vast amount of attending to sermons amounts to little more than solitary intellectual exercise—sermon criticism is often a spectator sport for Christians! Adults need to learn how to articulate their faith for themselves, and how to apply and work it out in their own lives, interacting with preachers and fellow church members. They can only do this fully as they engage in and reflect upon new activities, and as they work out human relationships in the light of their restored relationship with their heavenly Father. In most official church life there is hardly any space for such activity; there is little room for assumptions to be challenged, presuppositions to be punctured or true thought to begin. It is as people have the opportunity to put their own words together that they become conscious of their thoughts and realize new paths of behaviour.

5. Prepared and Structured Courses of Learning Should be Balanced with Immediacy of Response to Live Issues and Perceived Needs
Both Jesus and Paul were able to combine an awareness of the need for concerted, goal-oriented preaching and teaching (Mk 2.38; 6.7-13; Acts 19.9-10; 20.27) with the ability to seize impromptu opportunities (Mk 7.5-23; Acts 17.16-17). The preaching in many contemporary churches follows a poorly defined curriculum, often at the mercy of the private decisions of preachers. The use of a lectionary may help to cover a fairly broad range of topics dictated by the festivals of the Christian year. Some churches follow teaching plans which include and coordinate children's activities, while others devise their own sermon series and learning programmes. I would maintain that proper planning and design of teaching is essential to the health of the church, but that it should arise out of real research into the needs of the church, not the pet interests of preachers. It must be emphasized that teach-

ing should engage with the stage at which the learners are. This also implies that on-going programmes may sometimes have to be set aside in order to deal with unexpected and pressing questions.

b) Some Possibilities

One way in which a preacher might begin to respond to the issues raised so far might be to invite questions (or other contributions) from the congregation at the end of the usual sermon. Immediately a series of issues arise:

- Will questions be heard?
- Will there be too many questions/ how long will this take?
- Will there be no questions at all?
- Will there be inappropriate questions?

Some churches have been able to adopt this approach with the provision of certain facilities (like a roving microphone) and people capable of handling both questions and questioners.

Some churches have held over a question time until after the 'service' has finished. The implication of this arrangement, of course, is that the question-and-answer element is not quite as important or even as 'holy' as the 'real' sermon and other elements of the liturgy. An even weaker response has been to retain the sermon but to encourage small groups meeting during the week to discuss the contents of the Sunday sermon(s). This would indeed encourage some element of response to the sermon, but would minimize its immediacy (the preacher probably would not be present) and limit it to those able to attend such groups. It seems to me that one of the dangers facing churches today is that of compensating for the deficiencies of certain activities by adding new ones to the programme. The result is that meetings proliferate, administration increases and people become too busy. Thus the 'committed' people have little time for their families, friends and neighbours, while those who 'just come to church on Sunday' fail to experience much of true church life. If we perceive that there are weaknesses in our central church gatherings, then it is better to improve them than to supplement them.

The most effective dialogical or interactive preaching goes beyond some element of question or discussion at the end of a conventional sermon. I have participated in and conducted many teaching and training events which incorporate several of the following in addition to passages of monologue:

- Inviting and stopping for questions, answering them or providing for their subsequent answering.

- Allowing for a contribution or insight to be made which the preacher might not otherwise have included.

- Asking a church member to recount an experience of relevance to the subject (probably one already known to the preacher, and thus its relevance ensured).

- Getting the listeners into small 'buzz' groups of two or three to explore initial responses (ideas, feelings) to key issues being raised by the teacher, followed by a short time of feedback to the whole gathering of some of the these.

- Getting the listeners into groups of five or six for more extensive discussion of a subject, or to undertake a project (this could extend over a week or more) set by the teacher, again with feedback.

But can such interactive features be incorporated into the usual sermon 'slot'? Certain practical issues arise.

Seating arrangements may inhibit certain group activity. It is somewhat ironic that many churches have replaced pews with chairs and yet rarely take advantage of their movability during services. If the will is there, seating arrangements need not inhibit some congregational participation, though ultimately seating which facilitates congregational interaction is desirable.

The time needed for interactive preaching is considerable. However, time quickly passes if lively teaching combines with participatory learning. People will give time to what is interesting, helpful and involving. The preacher / teacher must be well prepared, and modern equipment may make a real contribution. Perhaps interactive preaching can begin in short bursts: during Lent (though not as a penance!) or during the month of, say, October, or perhaps once a month.

The number of people involved is significant. It is more difficult to incorporate elements of interactive preaching as the gathering increases in size. While there were certain occasions in the New Testament when large crowds heard teaching, we need to take seriously the high incidence of preaching and teaching of small to medium sized groups. Jesus' discipling focused on the twelve and the seventy,[44] and few of the early churches which met in people's homes would have numbered more than twenty to thirty, though in the cities locations may have been available for occasional larger gatherings.[45] Small churches have a definite advantage over large ones unless the large churches are prepared to be adventurous and divide into smaller gatherings for at least some teaching.

c) Some Possible Objections

Would not the introduction of contributions from the congregation clash with the liturgical elements of the rest of the gathering? A liturgy which minimizes the participation of the congregation to the singing of hymns and the occasional 'Amen' certainly will inhibit them from verbal response to preaching. Thus it is apparent that the theological considerations which I sought to expound earlier affect the whole gathering, and not simply the preaching. I can only point to the indications of congregational participation in the New Testament and ask whether churches with an such an inhibiting liturgical tradition might consider making changes on that basis. In fact, interactive preaching can lead into wonderfully creative prayer and praise.

Would some people feel intimidated or even driven away from church services by more interactive preaching? It is true that some people who attend church services are looking for a passive or reflective experience of God, and I would not want to disparage such an experience. However, I question the assumption that such rather individualistic experience should be the determining consideration in the regular gathering of God's people. I maintain that the corporate understanding of the church in the New Testament is so fundamental, and the need for effective preaching and teaching is so great, as to outweigh the contrary perceived needs of some. Churches which feel the need to continue to provide such experiences could still do so.

There is no doubt that I am advocating a radical change in church life. I realize that the changes which I advocate may seem difficult to achieve. They may require changes in more than the sermon 'slot.' They may encounter reluctance from preachers and from congregations. They may engender opposition. Any introduction of change requires sensitive handling —information and explanation, consultation, involvement, patience, leadership, and perhaps gradual introduction. Yet, if my theological advocacy of the interactive nature of true preaching and teaching has been true to the Scriptures and the Holy Spirit, then the question must become one of whether resistance to change will stifle the life and effectiveness that God wants to bring to the churches.

7

Conclusion

I hope that it will be clear that I am not renouncing the biblical mandate to preach God's word. On the contrary, it is because I believe passionately in it that I want to see it done yet more faithfully. The church is currently failing to be creative in its preaching, and thus failing to enable people to come to faith and to facilitate growth in discipleship. The resources available in the church are squandered if members believe that preaching is largely the responsibility of a special few who give sermons in religious settings. In order to communicate God's word effectively preachers must recognize the limitations of the monologue format of the sermon and encourage more interaction with their congregations. The new wine of preaching will burst the old skin of the sermon.

Notes

1   For example Klaus Runia, *The Sermon Under Attack* (Paternoster, 1983) pp 57-69; John Stott, *I Believe in Preaching* (Hodder & Stoughton, 1982) pp 60-64, 135-179; Nigel Watson, *Striking Home* (Epworth, 1987) pp 120-122; Donald Coggan, *The Sacrament of the Word* (Fount, 1987) pp 91-100; Sidney Greidanus, *The Modern Preacher and the Ancient Text* (Eerdmans/IVP, 1988) pp 157-187.

2   See Fred B Craddock, 'Preaching,' *The Anchor Bible Dictionary*, D N Freedman (ed) (Doubleday, 1992 vol V) p 453; R H Mounce, 'Preaching, Kerygma,' *Dictionary of Paul and his Letters* (IVP, 1993) pp 735-737. For further detail on the terminology see the articles on 'Gospel' and 'Proclamation' in the *New International Dictionary of Theology*, Colin Brown (ed) (Paternoster), vol 2 (1976), pp 107-115; vol 3 (1978), pp 44-68.

3   On Jesus as teacher see, for example, Robert Stein, *The Method and Message of Jesus' Teachings* (Westminster, 1978); R Reisner, 'Teacher,' *Dictionary of Jesus and the Gospels* (IVP, 1992) pp 807-11.

4   Many scholars think that the Sermon on the Mount (Mt 5.1-7.29) is a compilation of sayings, for example, R T France, *Matthew: Evangelist and Teacher* (Paternoster, 1990) pp 156-63; Donald A Hagner, *Matthew 1-13* (Word, 1993) pp 83. For a different view see D Carson, 'Matthew' in *The Expositor's Bible Commentary* (Zondervan, Vol 8, 1984) pp 122-125.

5   Many scholars would not understand the Johannine dialogues as traditions relating to real conversations, but see the plausible discourse analysis of conversation in P Cotterell and M Turner, *Linguistics and Biblical Interpretation* (SPCK, 1989) pp 257-292.

6   Stanley Stowers, 'Social Status, Public Speaking and Private Teaching; The Circumstances of Paul's Preaching Activity,' *Nov Test*, XXVI, 1 (1984), pp 59-82.

7   See Richard Longenecker, 'The Acts of the Apostles' in *The Expositor's Bible Commentary vol 9* (Zondervan, 1981) p 509.

8   Gerhard Lohfink, *Jesus and Community* (SPCK, 1985) p 99f.

9   See Robert Banks, *Paul's Idea of Community* (Peabody, MA: Hendrickson, 1994) pp 135-138. For another discussion of what happened in these assemblies, see Wayne Meeks, *The First Urban Christians* (Yale UP, 1983) pp 144-50.

10 Nigel Watson, *Striking Home* (Epworth, 1987) p 113f.

11 See William D Howden, 'Preaching,' *Encyclopaedia of Early Christianity*, Everett Ferguson (ed) (St James Press, 1990) pp 747-50.

12 See R D Sider, *The Gospel and its Proclamation* (Michael Glazier, 1983) p 91.

13 Martin Lloyd-Jones, *Preaching and Preachers* (Hodder & Stoughton, 1971) p 51.

14 K Runia, *The Sermon Under Attack*, p 32.

15 M Luther, *W A, Tischreden*, 4. 531. No 4812.

16 On Luther's preaching see Roland Bainton, *Here I Stand: A Life of Martin Luther* (Abingdon, 1950) pp 272-80.

17 J Calvin, *Commentary on Isaiah 55.11*.

18 J Calvin, *Institutes*, F L Battles (tr) (Westminster, 1960) IV.i.5, p 1017; cf IV.iii.1-2.

19 John H Leith, 'Calvin's Doctrine of the Proclamation of the Word and its Significance for Today' in *John Calvin and the Church; A Prism for Reform*, Timothy George (ed) (Westminster/John Knox, 1990) pp 206-229.

20 Against those who argue for a translation 'doing the truth,' see Andrew Lincoln, *Ephesians* (Word, 1990) p 259.

21 Calvin, *Institutes*, IV/1/5, p 1017.

22 T H L Parker, *Calvin's Preaching* (T & T Clark, 1992) p 43.

23 'Second Helvetic Confession (Confessio Helvetica Posterior)' (1566) in *Reformed Confessions of the Sixteenth Century*, Arthur Cochrane (ed), (1966) p 224.

24 K Barth, *The Doctrine of the Word of God (Church Dogmatics 1/1. 3 & 4)*, (T & T Clark, 1975) here p 98.

25 For the Reformers, something must happen to the listener: for Barth something must happen to the preaching. Klaas Runia, *Karl Barth and the Word of God* (TSF, 1977) pp 34-37.

26 See further K Barth, *Prayer and Preaching* (SCM, 1964) pp 69, 89.

27 K Barth *ibid* p 109.

28 For example G Ebeling, *The Nature of the Christian Faith* (Collins, 1961) p 184; Runia, (1977) pp 37-39.

29 James Daane, *Preaching With Confidence* (Eerdmans, 1980) p 15.

30 Martin Lloyd-Jones, *Preaching and Preachers* (Hodder & Stoughton, 1971) p 46f.

31 Alistair McFadyen, *The Call to Personhood: A Christian Theory of the Individual in Social Relationships* (Cambridge UP, 1990) pp 119-120.

32 *Ibid*, pp 48-61.

33 Gail O'Day, quoted in Stephen E Fowl & L Gregory Jones, *Reading in Communion* (SPCK, 1991) p 123.

34 Francis Watson, *Text, Church and World* (T & T Clark, 1994) p 115f.

35 *Ibid*, p 121.

36 Robert Banks, *Paul's Idea of Community* p 107-108.

37 It seems to me that this doctrine of the Spirit indwelling not just the preacher, but also the members of the church points towards a gathered view of the church. Interestingly, Luther seems to have hankered after a gathered church in a letter to Nicholas Hausman, 1523, and in the Preface to his *Deutsche Messe*, 1526.

38 James McClendon, *Ethics: Systematic Theology Volume I* (Abingdon, 1986); Stanley Hauerwas, *The Community of Character* (University of Notre Dame Press, 1981) and *The Peaceable Kingdom* (UNDP, 1983).

39 Ched Myers, *Who Will Roll Away the Stone?* (Orbis, 1994) p 26. See also John Navone, 'The Question-Raising Word of God,' *Theology*, 90 (1987), pp 288-293

40 J Moltmann, *The Trinity and the Kingdom* (SCM, 1981) p 192.

41 Ian A McFarland, 'Working from the Margins: an Evaluation of the Relationship between Authority and Responsibility in the Life of the Church,' *Modern Theology*, 12:3 July 1996, pp 301-319, here p 305.

42 David Buttrick, *Homiletic* (SCM, 1987) p 226.

43 An excellent study is still Anton Baumohl, *Making Adult Disciples* (Scripture Union, 1984).

44 For a good discussion of this issue, noting Jesus' focus on even smaller groups, see David Prior, *The Church in the Home* (Marshall Morgan and Scott, 1983) ch 2.

45 It is facile to dismiss the relevance of size of gathering in the New Testament as an accident of a historical development which led to large gatherings centred around the bishop, and to the construction of large basilicas. The large gathering in the dedicated church building continues to provide the dominant model of the successful modern (Western) church. But I want to ask on what grounds the social embodiment of the church in the New Testament may be set aside in favour of this subsequent model. However, this essential and intriguing subject must be left until another publication.

WYBOURN BLACK

Life on the wrong side of town

Between rounds, Herol Bomber Graham versus defending champion Kenny Bristol during their Commonwealth Lightweight Championship Boxing Match at Sheffield City Hall in 1981

Published by ACM Retro Ltd,
The Grange,
Church Street,
Dronfield,
Sheffield S18 1QB.

Visit ACM Retro at:
www.acmretro.com

Julian Antonio McKenzie asserts the moral right to be identified as the author of this work.

A catalogue record for this book is available from the British Library.

WYBOURN BLACK

Life on the wrong side of town

The Windsor - epicentre of Wybourn life in the 1970s and 1980s

Norfolk Park in full swing in 1981

CONTENTS

The infamous Roxy in the 1980s

ABC (later renamed Canon 1-2 Cinema) in 1987

"Honest and humorous. Definitely worth a read", *Richard Gear.*

INTRODUCTION

I'm no big time Charlie, I'm not showbiz either, there's nothing fake about me, even the tan's real.

What I will say about myself is I'm one of life's all round good Samaritans, honest, reliable, trustworthy, and a shoulder to cry on in your hour of need. (Give you the shirt off my back if I had to). In a nutshell, friend to many, foe too few.

I hail from Sheffield's notorious Wybourn estate - a place very close to my heart, a love affair that has lasted over 39 years and counting.

Now I know what you're thinking! Honest, reliable, trustworthy and off 'at Wybourn (no bloody way). Ha ha, yes way!

With a Dominican father, Jamaican mother and a name as regal as it sounds, this is my side of the story - the truth, the whole truth, and nothing but the truth, so help me mum…

No Blacks, No Irish, No Dogs

Well that's charming that is! They'd answered the call from their old colonial masters, an invitation of sorts from Queen Elizabeth herself. England, its arms outstretched across the Atlantic had promised a new way of life, a brand new home, and so they came, the young and the brave to be greeted by the old adage, 'No Blacks, No Irish, No Dogs'!

My mother left Orange Street, Jamaica, in July of 1956, a naïve young woman with her hopes and dreams packed tightly but neatly into a battered brown suitcase that had seen much better days. A heavy heart and tears were on the menu the day she boarded ocean liner Venezuela bound for Southampton, England, for a voyage of discovery.

Turning her back on the Motherland for how long, she wasn't sure. It would prove to be one of the biggest decisions of her life. One which would ultimately shape the rest of her time on Planet Earth.

After a two week voyage on the high seas, mum finally set foot onto British soil. London was her first destination, to stay with relatives who up until recently I never knew we had. After a brief pit stop in the capital it was off to Northampton to begin intense nurse training, a lifetime's ambition.

In 1958, training complete, Florence Nightingale (mum) landed a nursing position at the Fir Vale Royal Infirmary in Sheffield, the Northern General as it's universally known today. Mum's infatuation with the Steel City had started when she used to visit a friend who had made the identical journey as her on the Venezuela. Having gone their separate ways in Southampton they vowed to stay in touch.

Mum travelled to London as we know and her friend headed up north to Sheffield. Mum has since told me of how she was mesmerised by the landscape and nightlife of the Steel City - she visited frequently. London at the time just wasn't her thing.

Unbeknown to her it was one of these frequent visits that had already caught the attention of another newly inducted resident of Sheffield.

Now the old man, hang on I think a bit of respect is due here! My dad arrived in England on a large tidal wave of enthusiasm in 1954 from Dominica, a French speaking island in the heart of the West Indies. On arrival it didn't take him long to find employment as a bus conductor and later driver with Sheffield Yorkshire Transport, where he would eventually clock up more than thirty years of public service. A stickler for looking smart and being well turned out, dad would spend countless hours ironing razor sharp creases into his shirts and trousers. Whether it be for work or play, everything had to be bonafide perfect. His secret to the perfect crease was water and brown paper. With his own unique style in place, dad topped things off with a side parting Moses would have struggled to emulate.

A whirlwind romance ensued between the two, not long after wedding bells chimed. If dad was the king of heartbreakers, his heir apparent would inherit the gift from the greatest teacher of them all.

Enoch's Offspring

Now you can laugh if want to, but I actually thought I had a great Uncle Enoch! Let me explain... Every so often when my behaviour wasn't at its very best, mum would say Uncle Enoch won't be happy with you or Uncle Enoch is watching you.

Turns out Great Uncle Enoch was non other than that fine upstanding politician Enoch Powell, you know the one, the Rivers of Blood and all that. Powell had given his infamous speech against a backdrop of civil unrest and tension amongst social communities concerned about Britain's immigration policies of the day. Repatriation was his subtle way of saying 'go back home', and with a cash incentive to do just that, the offer was put firmly on the table.

Page Hall Arrival

Now I have it on good authority that mum had given birth to a beautiful baby boy (her little soldier today), weighing in at 9lb 6oz - I was her big brown barrel of fun, heartbreaker the second. Mum and dad now resided at Idsworth Road, Page Hall. The family was now complete, or so I was led to believe because a year later mum did it again, giving birth to another big brown barrel of fun who had subsequently stolen all of my thunder, and would continue to do so for many more years to come. My little sister (yuki).

As three became four, it was pretty obvious our accommodation needs were much greater than ever before. Mum orchestrated a move onto a housing estate that was going through a transitional period of refurbishment, but before we could move into the new improved dwelling on said estate, we moved across the city to Sheffield Hyde Park Flats.

Say what you want about those flats, most people do beginning in F and ending in dump. I found life as a young kid there pretty cool.

It was only years later that my perceptions changed and I found the complex grey and uninspiring; rows and rows of slab concrete ruthlessly piled on top of each other rising as far as the naked eye could see. Add to that the nauseating views of a city deep in decline, then maybe the perceptions people had were truly justified. I know as I got older my overall view did change somewhat, beginning in F and ending in dump!

Home was eight floors up on Dacer Row. As you walked through the front door you were confronted by stairs that led down to the basement living quarters, bedrooms, bathroom etc etc. The living room overlooked the middle and top half of Wybourn estate, our soon to be new home in waiting; it also overlooked the Hyde Park dog track. I reckon mum and dad saved a few bob on the electricity on race nights, because the floodlights lit up the living room like a beacon. On the other side of the flat was my bedroom which overlooked Spital Hill, Brightside, Wincobank and most of the industrial heart of Sheffield.

The one thing I didn't need to get me up for school in the morning was an alarm clock, Sheffield Forgemasters saw to that. Every morning between 3am and 4am I'd be rudely awaken by the giant hammer press that would operate, try as I might to ignore the intrusion Forgemasters came out on top every time.

Within the flats was a small shopping precinct with a launderette, hairdressers, supermarket and newsagent, and if my memory serves me well, Bradshaw's fruit and veg.

By now I was attending Wybourn Nursery School, but cannot for the life of me remember anything about it bar the occasional flashback of hanging my coat up with the traditional ladybird picture on the peg alongside my name.

The nursery was next to the junior quarters which I attended for a further eight years, before the big one. Lifelong friendships were forged at juniors, friendships that have stood the test of time, they read like a who's who of Wybourn hierarchy.

The headmaster, Mr Noakes, was a jovial old sod, with hands, in my experience, that could be as lethal as Bruce Lee.

During break times we were given free milk, I really detested it. To this very day the thought of drinking cold milk sends a cold shiver down the length of my spine. I mustn't forget the small pink straw too. To accompany the cow's poison we could purchase huge brick thick chocolate biscuits with a shortbread base that tasted like they were made in heaven. I haven't tasted anything like them since.

One Christmas I auditioned for a part in Wybourn Juniors adaptation of Mary and Joseph. After a successful read through I got the part of one of the three wise men. (Ahh the smell of the grease paint!)

On the night of the performance I was officially a bag of nerves; in front of me was a full house in the school gym expecting a performance of Olivier proportions. Unfortunately for me what happened next has gone down in Wybourn school folklore.

As I was approaching the stage from the rear of the gym my cloak was trailing on the floor, a bit like a posh wedding gown. All of a sudden I was catapulted backwards as one of the other wise men stepped on the tail of the cloak. After struggling back into position and regaining my composure I made my way to the front of the stage. I only had a few lines to say but proceeded to fluff them all the same. Not only that, I forgot to give the baby Jesus his Christmas prezzy. Denzil Washington and Samuel L Jackson needn't have worried, my promising career on stage and screen was well and truly over.

Mum was in the audience that night, at least I think she was! Yes I'm almost certain the dark skinned lady with her head in her hands was indeed mum.

Andrew Lloyd Webber didn't hang around for long either, he even forgot to leave his card.

Meanwhile life on the flats was pretty cool, I made lots of friends with the other kids that lived on the landing and realised it would be tough to say goodbye. One of our favourite games was knock and run, I can imagine how the irate occupants felt every time they climbed the stairs to answer the door.

In the summer months we'd take a lift to the ground floor and play next to the huge telecom building just off Whites Lane. Every day there would be an endless fleet of canary yellow vans going about their telecommunications business, Busby was raking it in!

With that year's summer at its end it was time for me to move up a year in school and that meant the big boys' playground, and girls of course.

Us juniors used to dream of playing football with the older boys for whom many were older brothers of pals. Staring through the railings at the cool kids became an everyday event. The big question was, could I myself live up to their expectations?

I didn't want summer of '76 to end, not now, not ever, but in its final days it was time to make the move that would shape the rest of my life.

Ain't No Turning Back...

Like Reagan and Carter we were in hot pursuit of our belongings, it was the day of the move (Hyde Park to Wybourn) and the removal van driver had shot off the grid as though his life depended on it.

After a high speed three minute chase, dad picked up the vapour trail. The driver, by now satisfied he'd broken all land speed records and taken the chequered flag, had come to an abrupt stop - we were here.

On close inspection it looked like any other ordinary suburban street, but as we ejected from the car dad's eyes lit up like that of a child on Christmas morning. We followed his gaze to a majestic looking building in front of us and directly opposite our new home; it was a pub, the Windsor Hotel. It looked very stately like, sticking out like a throbbing sore thumb amongst rows of ordinary homes. At the side of that was another building that seemed to polish things off nicely for dad, a bookmakers; a small one but a bookmakers all the same. Well at least mum knew where she could find him of an afternoon. She'd also have to wrestle her share of his pay packet too.

As we made our way through the front door of number 52 Southend Road I shot off in the direction of the stairs in a desperate bid to lay claim to the biggest and best bedroom. In the end I settled on the room at the front, with the pub and the betting shop in plain view. Whilst taking in the new surroundings I noticed out of the corner of my left eye a building we hadn't noticed on the way in. It was double take time as I caught sight of what looked like a medieval castle surrounded by huge walls.

This turned out to be Sheffield Manor Castle grounds and the building in question was once the home of Mary Queen of Scots. I say home, but she was actually imprisoned there by Queen Elizabeth I who saw the Scottish Queen as a threat to her very existence and throne (history on the doorstep along with the empties!) Having found the courage to do a little exploring for myself after a couple of days unpacking, I discovered St Oswald's School, a chip shop, corner shop, newsagents and at the top of the road a cemetery (a handy thing to have on the Wybourn by all accounts).

During the first few days of our move, we spent most of our evenings in front of the TV, *Crossroads* was a favourite of mum's along with *On The Buses* and *Man About The House*.

Dad was a big fan of *The Good Old Days* and the *Dick Emery Show*, he was an even bigger fan of a Thames Television sitcom that would divide opinion amongst TV viewers the length and breadth of the UK. It would also provide a huge slice of irony that wouldn't be lost on us as a family in our new surroundings.

Love Thy Neighbour starred Jack Smethhurst and Rudolph Walker and told the story of a white working class couple's initial shock of having gained new neighbours who happened to be black.

Feelings were still running high amongst the country's inhabitants fearful of the sudden influx of immigrants entering the UK; the show was seen (mainly in TV land) as a way of defusing a volatile situation with laughter. But not everyone was laughing - the show was slammed by viewers and critics alike, its racial overtones being called into question with each episode.

'Sambo', 'nig-nog', 'snowflake' and 'honky' were the kind of incendiary words regularly used in the show which aired from 1972 to 1976.

Talking of neighbours, our new ones were mainly families with children in the same age bracket as me and my little sister, the only exception being a dear old man who lived next door. He didn't venture out much, nor did he receive many visitors and he definitely wasn't the green fingered type judging by the undergrowth that loomed large above the garden fence. He was a quiet man who lived and died at number 54.

I wasn't a big fan of dogs at this juncture having nearly had my own arm chewed off outside Bill's Shop directly at the side of school, clearly one tin of Pedigree Chum wasn't enough that day.

A couple of the neighbours did have dogs, but as time passed by we got pretty used to each other; there were two Labradors that lived at number 44, one black and one white, and if the K9's could live together in harmony then there was hope for us all.

Now the odd thing about the other kids on the street (sorry) cul de sac, was that I didn't know any of them. Ok I know I was the new boy, but what I mean is not one of them attended Wybourn School; Manor Lodge and St Oswald's were the popular choices here, one of the boys even ventured out to Shirecliffe on the other side of Sheffield to attend Herries - did their parents know something mine didn't? On a personal note it was an unforgettable '76! Moving home, endless summer days, day trips to ladybird infested seaside resorts, a West Indian cricket uprising at the Oval, and bad boy Johnny was turning rotten to the core with the Sex Pistols!

In my first term at Wybourn middle school the gang found themselves back together again. We'd been together since potty training and had established an unbreakable unit amongst ourselves. Brothers and sisters in arms. Here we found a difference in teaching styles because they (the teachers) seemed well up for it (trouble that is!); it's even possible they'd spent the entire six week break getting ready to do battle with another generation of Wybourn's finest.

Looking back I felt sorry for one particular teacher, because we gave her such a hard time, there was some real characters in the classroom including myself, and it was just bad luck she'd inherited a room full of jokers.

Her gold watch should have been handed over years before. Our classroom was twinned with another classroom but there was no concrete walls separating the masses, it was a strong plastic curtain on rails, top and bottom, with handles on either end to open and close.

During lessons you could hear what the other teacher was talking or shouting about, I guess the school had run out of Government funds to finish the whole thing off. During one particular lesson one lad was being reprimanded when all of a sudden he rose from his chair and punched his teacher in the chest. The teacher flew across the table. I can't remember what was said, but he was the quietest of the bunch who had suddenly turned on the teacher. Within seconds of the incident the plastic curtain opened from the other side and another teacher, who would go on to be a legend in his own right in later years, grappled our mate to the floor. The pupil was promptly dragged by the scruff of the neck across the playground to the headmaster's office.

A few of the girls (when they had stopped screaming) tended to the teacher who had taken the mandatory count and was helped over to a nearby chair.

As far as head teachers go our new head was your typical Mr Chips type; he was tall, he was thin, his specs perched themselves on the bridge of his nose and he wore an ill-fitting grey suit with more creases in it than Barbara Cartland.

School became a distant memory for me during the weekend, I swept the whole education trip under the carpet and banished all books under the bed.

Saturdays and Sundays became my own precious release. Mum would treat us to a picture show at the Classic Cinema in Fitzalan Square, most of them Disney classics, *Dumbo, Freaky Friday* starring a young Jodie Foster and most of the *Herbie* trilogy, I also recall seeing another film featuring Foster with a cast of children playing all the lead roles, *Bugsy Malone*.

After each showing, having stuffed ourselves silly with popcorn and huge hot dogs, we'd drag mum off to the Castle Market making a swift beeline toward the broken biscuit stall.

I knew my way round the market like the back of my hand but on a few occasions, only a few mind, Castle Market used to fill me with dread. Every so often, mainly on Saturdays, I'd have to help mum with the shopping (like a good son should I may add!); we'd head straight over to Mumtaz's continental stall to stock up on all the West Indian delights that were on offer. Clever man that Mumtaz, he saw the potential and he took it.

He drew huge crowds with his green bananas, yams, salt fish, assorted peppers and tropical fruits. The Caribbean ex pats would gather and barter over the prices and have the chance to natter at length in the home-grown dialects they'd left behind thousands of miles away.

And in the middle of all this was me; I found it amusing yet impossible to understand, I was fast becoming a proper Yorkshire man with a Geoffrey Boycott twang that was coming on at a rate of knots.

Hustle and tussle over with, mum and I and sometimes my sister would walk through Sheaf Market and over the bridge to catch a bus opposite Granelli's just off Duke Street. You had to be quick on the draw though, with your hand ready to stop your preferred ride home as the buses would fly round the corner at breakneck speeds. The number 93 to Woodthorpe, the number 92 to Woodhouse, and last but not least the number 56 to Wybourn, the Promised Land.

God Save The Queen

There were quite a few raised eyebrows when mum decided to up sticks and move across the city to Wybourn; there was great concern amongst friends who thought it not the smartest of moves.

But the one thing mum possessed in abundance were balls, big brass ones, no one was going to dictate to her where and how she should live. Besides, what did they expect, white hoods and burning crosses? Wybourn's a lot of things but Mississippi it ain't.

The six week holidays were fast approaching once more and my first year at Wybourn middle was nearly over - one down, three to go.

Britain was in the grip of Jubilee fever, the Queen's reign reaching its milestone of 25 years and the country was ready to celebrate on the grandest of scales. In our cul de sac (or keyhole as it was better known now because it resembled the shape of a... yeah you guessed it) we'd been planning a party for its residents leaving everyone else on the outside looking in.

I found this really unfair especially as my best friend at school lived at number 24, out of the jurisdiction so to speak; but we got round that little problem with relative ease. A huge trestle table was erected and put down the centre of the keyhole draped in several white table cloths; the bunting and Union Jacks had been deployed a couple of days beforehand. Most of the windows were either draped in red, white and blue, or had a huge picture of the Queen taped to them. Our house had neither, dad was having none of that, after 23 years he still saw himself as a guest a stranger on someone else's turf.

Now getting back to my friend at number 24, there was no invitation forthcoming so we hatched a plan to gate crash HRH's party. It was simple really, no one was locking their doors in the days when you could do that sort of thing, plus there would be plenty of people milling about. My friend waited in our living room watching TV and waited for the signal, after several attempts trying to replicate the Tarzan call I gave it up as a bad job and opted for a small brick against the window. Matey would then position himself in the garden and wait for the blitzkrieg of food.

Sausage rolls, pork pies and thinly cut sandwiches were launched over the privet hedge with deadly accuracy, the jelly would have to be cleaned off the windows at a later date. The day and our mission was a resounding success, we'd covered all bases and covered our tracks. And if I was caught in the act?

Well I would have passed the bizarre ritual as an ancient Caribbean custom. Oh come on, who's going to question that?

The closest I ever came to seeing the Queen was when her royal visit to Sheffield came to an end and she sped through on the Parkway to her next royal engagement. I was hoisted on the shoulders of one of the older Wybourn lads and watched her gleaming white glove wave to the flag waving crowds.

It was all over within seconds, but as a young lad I was thrilled to bits.

It was a solemn voice that came over the speakers of our brand new Philips record player with the Perspex lid (Wigfalls buy of the week) that broke the news that Elvis Presley, the King of rock'n' roll, was dead.

It was mid August and I was gearing up for another term at Wybourn middle school, my second year.

Having given our first year teacher the run around and a one way ticket to the teaching retirement rest home we were ready for our next victim.

We were brash, we were arrogant and minus the Ali shuffle we couldn't wait to get it on - the magnificent twelve ride again.

In round one we suffered the lowest of blows below the belt when we were paired with someone with a fearsome reputation to protect, she made light work of cleaning up Dodge City, bringing us to heel within seconds of us walking through the door.

Of course the girls in the class loved every minute of it, seeing the boys on their knees made her an instant heroin, a role model for all the would be bra burners in the school. Any bad behaviour in her classroom would be seriously dealt with, which entailed being frogmarched to the corner of the room to stand arms out stretched. In truth the shorter the arms the better off you were. I've always had long arms, so for me with a wing span that rivalled that of a giant albatross, it was a nightmare.

In the playground where we played 27 a side football during break times, the slope wouldn't have looked out of place on BBC2's *Ski Sunday* introduced by the late David Vine. The slant was, and still is, unbelievable. If you found yourself behind in a game it was truly an uphill struggle to get back into the game.

A Wybourn school craze was sweeping through the playground during the term called The Ninety Nine, forget the ice cream cone with flake on top, this was a million miles away from that.

It was some sort of initiation test dreamt up by one of the older boys in the third year that spiralled out of control, and would have worried parents jamming the school switchboard wanting to know what happened to poor little Johnny.

Your sleeves were rolled up to reveal the top half of your wrist and the test would be performed thus so: the index finger of no one in particular would rub your arm with the nail of said digit ninety nine times with as much vigour as they could muster, leaving a nasty red rash like scar on your arm.

With the skin rubbed into oblivion a pinch of salt would be inducted into the wound, this would then scab over in time meaning you were now a member of an exclusive club, what club no one knew, but it opened up a fair few doors with the cool kids in school.

It didn't take long for the school to clamp down on the activity, branding it dangerous and unhygienic. I had the process done to me twice because no one believed I'd had it done in the first place, what with my skin colouring, so I gritted my teeth again, this time in front of an audience.

Having plenty of witnesses has failed me once or twice later in life, believe me!

If it wasn't bad enough having to deal with a teacher's unorthodox methods and discipline, I thought things couldn't get any worse for us until we were introduced to the latest school offering of keeping order, The Three P's.

'Perfect Peter prefects' were unleashed midway through the term, the eyes and ears of teachers who wished to finish their coffee and custard creams in relative peace.

Safe in the knowledge that Peter would grass anyone up for the sake of a pat on the head, left the teachers feeling rather smug. The Peters thought it was great too, having the responsibility of keeping order in the absence of the Führers, but they soon started to throw in their badges when one Peter took a few too many punches to the jaw outside Bill's shop.

Within a week the teachers were leaving half finished brews once again to deal with the latest commotion kicking off in the playground.

World Cup year had always been special, and this year was no exception, it was my first tournament and I couldn't wait for it to start.

I loved the beautiful game, it was the one thing that brought me and the other lads in the keyhole together playing endless games of football on the playing fields directly behind our houses.

We played well after the sun went down, and it was only until an assortment of mothers voices would shout us all in that the games would end.

Argentina was the unlikeliest of venues to host such a tournament, given its problems on the human rights front and a military dictatorship that took no prisoners. England had failed to qualify again, but in their absence were those plucky Scots who were talking up their chances of bringing the trophy home, with anyone who would stop to listen.

I was starting to get my own way in front of the TV now, we both were, my sister and I; on Saturday mornings you'd find us on the sofa watching cartoon classics such as the *Hair Bear Bunch, Scooby Doo, Top Cat,* and the *Pink Panther Show.* I'd also started watching another kids' favourite from America called *B.J. and the Bear.* B.J. McCay was a young trucker who drove a red and white rig across America with his sole companion bear, who was a chimp (you still with me?) Each week they'd cross county lines and come up against a host of corrupt sheriffs intent on destroying the town and its good people, McCay and the bear would often stick around to help until it was time to move on, a bit like the *Littlest Hobo,* which I enjoyed watching too.

But my all time favourite was the *Beachcombers,* a family run logging company in British Columbia in Canada. My favourite character was Jesse the native American Indian who worked for the loggers and would get up to all sorts of mischief.

In the evenings dad was back at the helm in front of the TV, I used to get up and make the long trek across the living room to change the channel for him, no remote control yet don't forget. Which meant it was a fucking nightmare when he wanted to channel hop!

The big film of the year had to be *Grease,* mum took me and my sister to see it at the ABC theatre on Angel Street in town.

I remember the day as if it were yesterday because we queued up for two showings before we got anywhere near the front, that's about three hours. John Travolta was box office gold dust back then and coming off the back of *Saturday Night Fever,* he had the world at his (dancing) feet.

Meanwhile the school term was nearly over and we lads couldn't wait to trade our teacher in for a newer model. The towel had been thrown in months ago, her iron grip winning the day or term, by a country mile. By the way Argentina won the World Cup that year, and some bird was born in a test tube! Whatever next?

I Belong To Wales

Imagine, an English first name, Italian middle name, a Scottish surname, Jamaican mother and a Dominican father and me on my way to Wales. My ancestry dates back to slavery, but someone was clocking up the air miles big time.

The new third term is the one I won't be forgetting in a hurry, remembered if for nothing else but the rumoured infidelities of some school staff who will remain nameless. But more of that later.

Nothing gave me greater pleasure on the way to school than to slip into Bill's shop and load up with as many sweets and chocolate as my money would allow. Curly Wurlys, Highland Toffee bars and Sherbert Refreshers were top of the most wanted list, and if I had enough left after that little treasure trove, I'd finish things off with a 'twenty pence mix up'.

The bags were already made up, which saved Bill a lot of time and trouble and more often than not I'd have to delve deep into that bag to fish out all the Black Jacks. Not because I was offended by them, but simply because I couldn't stand liquorice.

I picked up a new nickname that year, that of Pele, the greatest footballer on the planet (him not me!) and if truth be told it was a damn sight better than the ones I'd picked up in recent months.

I was on a real hiding to nothing when American mini-series *Roots* hit British screens, trust me. The name Pele was given to me by a classmate, one of the magnificent twelve who still greets me with the same name some thirty years after I was unofficially christened with it.

My lessons were going really well, I was a good listener and very attentive up to a point then the distractions would kick in. But there was one lesson that wouldn't be afforded any of my attention, not a jot.

Thursday morning was the one day I set aside for being really ill, not well enough to attend class, stomach bugs, chest pains, vomiting and diarrhoea whatever it took to stay away from school. For Thursday mornings lesson was the only one that made me run for the hills... swimming.

I hated everything Sheffield Sheaf Valley baths stood for (swimming mainly). I hated the smell, its location and its very being. Sandwiched between a very dark and grey Pond Street Bus Station, and equally dark and grey Sheffield Midland Train Station, Sheaf Valley represented everything a living nightmare should look like.

Those three or four steps leading up to the double doors was on par with a meeting with the devil himself, I wasn't afraid of the water! Far from it, I just didn't see the point of learning to swim.

In my defence, I've never fallen off any boats, nor have I or the rubber duck run into any difficulty in the bath so why?

Well I've got news for you Wybourn Middle School, that 25 yard certificate I obtained all those years ago, I was walking on the bottom of the pool the whole time. There what have you got to say about that then? The other thing I hated about those sessions in the pool do you really know how long it takes to dry a full head of afro hair in time for double maths?

Morning school assembly was always a riotous affair, we'd file into the main hall class by class taking our seats like some expectant audience at a rock concert. We'd kick things off with the Lord's Prayer, heads bowed giggling and laughing like mischievous young chimps and pulling girls' pigtails for added amusement.

The head would then plod on through his lengthy itinerary for the day before letting Wolfgang Amadeus Fryer, the over exuberant music teacher, thrash the keys of the school piano.

Fryer was a giant of a man with a physique that would put any would be Mr Universe to shame, a strapping six foot something of brain and brawn.

Man Fryer, as he was affectionately known, took the job very seriously. I didn't particularly enjoy his lessons but his full on approach had to be seen to be believed. During his lessons he wouldn't be seen without his trademark long piece of bamboo cane, which would be used to point to the musical notes that were projected onto the white walls of the assembly room.

Man Fryer was every inch the mad conductor, and I mean that in the nicest possible way.

It was one of those school assemblys that I learned of a school trip to Wales, Llandudno to be precise, and everyone was given the opportunity to go. We were given a letter to give to our respective parents, the consent form was attached to the bottom. If your parents gave you the go ahead all that was needed then was a signature from either mum or dad.

I took mine home in hope rather than expectation because the whole trip would cost a mind blowing £45, a lot of dough in late 1970s Britain. Mum thought it was great idea for me to see the world, even if it was only over the border and down the M1, at least I think it was.

I was given a small green payment booklet that was stamped every time money was paid in. It took more than the allotted nine weeks to pay the £45 because money was tight back then so some weeks I didn't pay, couldn't pay, but I knew mum wouldn't let me down. On completion my book was stamped in huge red letters, 'paid in full', I was on my way to the valleys.

I didn't really know what to expect from Llandudno, I was so used to the northern way of life in England, the smoke and the smog of a city fighting to survive. I didn't know anything else, and if you're brought up thinking the Tinsley cooling towers were part of the seven wonders, then it was high time you found out things for yourself.

Needless to say I fell in love with the principality as soon as my feet touched down on Welsh soil, the rolling hillsides, the lush green green grass and the never ending line of trees that forged into a landscape that was just breath taking (that Tom Jones was bang on the money that's for sure!) When we arrived in Llandudno I fell even deeper in love with the country - and this was just a fraction of what they, the Welsh, had to offer. The peace and tranquillity of the place was sublime.

That didn't last for long though on our arrival, there was some real characters on the trip and I was pleasantly surprised that so many of them were allowed to make the trip, after all they were representing the school. But I guess back home school was breathing a huge sigh of relief, for five days at least.

The Bedford Hotel was to be my temporary home and I couldn't wait to get unpacked and out there.

I forget who I roomed with, but we the lads used to congregate in one room or the other to hatch our plans for mayhem and mischief.

The coach driver who transported us over the border would be driving us to different locations for the next few days and this was as much a holiday for him as it was for us. He was a bit of a jack the lad, everybody liked him including one of our female teachers. She sat directly at the side of the driver acting as some sort of guide, she never stopped laughing at his jokes and one liners the whole trip, which was strange because she was really reserved, but they got on like a house on fire, so where was the harm in that?

Meanwhile I was enthralled by Llandudno, we visited castles, monuments and places of interest that tied in with the trip, we used to walk a mile ahead of the other teachers who would frantically try to keep up.

I've kept my memories of Llandudno in the memory bank, and I've always promised myself a return to that little piece of paradise that captivated me at such an early age. And just like General MacArthur, I shall indeed return. Come Monday morning my Welsh affair was over, but I was always eager to rekindle my love for Llandudno and its people.

Playing football on the sea front, the sounds of the passing trams outside the hotel bedroom window of an evening, and the fresh clean air of an untamed wilderness seemed a million miles away now I was back on the Wybourn.

Turns out while we were away the rumours surrounding two of our more flirty members of teaching staff hit the school headlines after allegedly being caught in a compromising position in an empty classroom.

He was tall, (not so) dark, and devilishly handsome (that's the girls view by the way!). His sparring partner well she was easily one of the most attractive looking teacher I'd ever come across.

And so my friends another term done, and one more to go. I spent the run up to the summer holidays fooling around with my mates, playing football in the yard, and running away from the boy with the glass eye.

Whistle Test

If I were to tell you that Nazi Germany, and in particular Herman Goering's elite Luftwaffe air squadron, were responsible for my musical identity, you'd probably be right in thinking I was off my nut on any number of banned substances.

But I have to tell you that it's perfectly true, because out of the rubble and ruin of a city I'd never even heard of before, came a steely determination to rebuild, prosper, and succeed.

I didn't have any records of my own to boast about, but there was plenty of hits and misses in my mum and dad's collection of 45s and 33s to play around with, but nothing really hit the back of the net.

There were some great labels in there including Decca, Sun, Calypso, Motown and huge collection of Trojan. I can remember playing George McCrae's 'Rock Your Baby' album a lot and Boney Ms seminal 'Night Flight To Venus', but apart from that I stayed well clear. The radio was where my real passion for music started in the late '70s, the new wave scene was in its infancy and the tracks that were being championed by ace DJ John Peel were pretty decent. Glam rock was forgotten by then, and punk never really got a chance to spread its wings, or take off, so it was down to the new kids to set the records straight. One of my favourites was 'Oliver's Army' by Elvis Costello and the Attractions, a really catchy number that did very well in the charts as I recall.

Other favourites included 'Roxanne' by the Police, Lene Lovich's 'Lucky Number' and Ian Dury's classic, 'Hit Me With Your Rhythm Stick'.

During the summer holidays I did the usual thing of kicking my now familiar orange football around, either in the garden much to the annoyance of mum because her roses took a tremendous pounding, or on the playing fields with the older boys off the keyhole.

Which brings me nicely to our dear neighbours at number 50 who were and still are a really nice family, mum was a divorcee and lived with her three children, two daughters and a son who was the same age as me. We got on really well and again it was the beautiful game that brought us two together, we used to head the ball backwards and forwards to each other over the garden fence, the first to lose control of the ball lost a point and we'd play that for hours on end, only taking a break when it was snap time.

I lost most of the games because I couldn't get any power in my headers because my afro would cushion the ball when it came to me. We had some great times him and me and in turn he introduced me to some of his other friends who became good friends of mine growing up.

In time his mum met another man who just happened to be a fellow bus driver like my dad, and the two of them got on really well too. Our neighbours new love interest had a great party piece that we found really funny, he used to drive his bus home and park it in the keyhole or at the end of the road when he came home for a break.

He wouldn't take it to the depot and collect his own car, he'd just cut the middle man out and arrive home on a double decker blocking out the view and the sun. It was a sad day when they decided to move house as the family was getting bigger, but they didn't venture far away moving to the relatively new Skye Edge housing project a mere five minutes away if that. I went to visit them once and couldn't believe the view they had from their living room window, you could even see downtown Bramall Lane, although I suspect there was some money knocked off the price for that (spoil of view!)

One summer's evening I tuned into the John Peel show on Radio One to be confronted by a unique but familiar sound , I'd heard that type of tune before on many of the Trojan records that sat proudly on our record shelf, but this was a raw unpolished sound that had me hooked. Even though I'd tuned in a minute or so after the record had started my immediate mission was to find out who the band were.

At the end of the record, right on cue Peel with his now familiar deadpan voice introduced me, and the rest of the United Kingdom to the Specials.

I had no idea what they looked like, nor where they came from, but I knew I had to hear the record again from start to finish to make this a leading contender for the first record I would buy.

It later transpired that they hailed from the city of Coventry in the Midlands, and were one of the founding members of the new British ska movement.

To be honest I couldn't wait to get away. This was going to be my last full term at Wybourn middle school, one step away from a brand new start.

Don't get me wrong, the school had been good to me, but not quite good enough, let's just say they tolerated me, I just couldn't settle down, a trait that would follow me round like a shadow.

My new form teacher that year was the football mad Mr Lockwood, complete with dodgy all in one blue tracksuit, regulation whistle hung round his neck, and the magical cup of coffee that would never spill in any given situation including having a kick around in the yard at break times with the lads.

This was a first for me and the rest of the gang because we'd gone through the previous three years with female form teachers for company. Lockwood would be the ultimate test of how far we could push someone's buttons to the limit.

There was an air of excitement that term, at the end of it a whole new experience lay ahead in the form of secondary school, new teachers, new friends, new location.

My grades by now were good to average, I wasn't excelling in anything in particular, but I was showing a lot of promise when the mood took me, my reading was good and that was part due to the colour coded system that was put into place before we arrived at junior level.

Each colour had three bands, thin, thick and double, and these were stuck to the books we read, if you're reading wasn't up to scratch you'd be given a thin banded book, if you were an average reader you got a thick band, and if you were a really smart cookie you were handed a double bander.

The colours white, red, blue, green and yellow signified the level you were at, black was the top of the tree, the benchmark to which you had to aspire.

I was thick black (no jokes please!) for a month or two before hitting the jackpot, and being handed a double banded black book.

Games lessons took on a whole new competitive edge with Mr Lockwood and it showed when we played five a side in the school yard, he used to knock us off the ball with all the passion of a professional hard man, sometimes forgetting we were eleven years old and the surface was concrete.

When we took on other schools in the eleven a side format we'd walk up the hill onto the Sky Edge playing fields, and there in the distance my old stomping ground, Hyde Park Flats.

My relationship with Lockwood wasn't great, don't ask me why because I wouldn't be able to tell you even now. I spent more time in the corridor than I did at my desk. When he had the ball at his feet I became his star pupil, but with a piece of chalk in his hand forget it.

Girls hadn't really bothered me up to this point, but there was one particular young female I had a huge crush on since infant school, we'd come a long way since the days of building blocks and sandpits and I guess the moment we met I fancied the training pants of her. She was the prettiest girl in our year if not the whole school, and I was besotted, I used to follow her around like some love sick puppy just watching her every move, but I strongly deny whole heartedly of ever being the founding member of the Stalkers Association!

Having purchased the Specials debut single for the princely sum of seventy five pence, or there abouts from Woolies, my attention turned to seeing them in action.

The chance came one evening when they were due to guest on BBC2's flagship music show, *The Old Grey Whistle Test*. The programme had recently taken a huge boot up the backside for ignoring the new music that was happening all around them, the establishment grabbed Bob Harris and co by the balls and squeezed hard until the new world order of musicians were invited to perform on the show.

Out went the likes of Captain Beefheart, Roxy Music, Janis Ian and Super tramp and in their place the brand new sounds of Blondie, Talking Heads, Squeeze, XTC and of course the Specials.

They were about to showcase their new single, a cover of Dandy Livingston's 'Rudy A Message To You', and the word on the street was that these boys were good and were being lorded in the highest of musical circles.

Well I have to tell you as soon as the harmonica kicked off the live performance I made my mind up there and then I was a huge fan and this was the band I wanted to follow. Of course I'd heard the track before a million times over by Dandy but the Specials made it their own, and without sounding disrespectful to Mr Livingstone, wiped the floor with his version of things all ends up.

Lead singer Terry Hall was the one member of the band that reeled me in, his performance faultless. Not only that, the way he presented himself during the performance was nothing short of genius. Dressed mainly in black apart from white socks and white cravat with black polka dots, Hall had this audience of one sat on the sofa at number 52 Southend Road, Sheffield in a feeding frenzy for more.

Within a few weeks of the *Whistle Test* performance I had obtained most of the gear, the rude boy wardrobe, the black monkey boots were from Timpson's on the High Street and when I picked them out mum's face was a picture, but she didn't bang on about how crude they were, she just handed over the money. When I tried them on the girl in the shop asked me to walk up and down in them as they used to do, but I didn't walk in them though, I strutted.

Footwear sorted it was down the escalator into the Hole In The Road and into the ground floor boys' department of C & A for a pair of ill-fitting trousers.

Hall had worn his trousers high up to his waist supported by braces but I drew the line at those because I would have looked a right tit wearing them, the trousers met the boots with a glimpse of white sock in between.

That task was easier than I first imagined, all I had to do was make sure the waist size was right, and the inside leg measurement wrong.

The new look was completed when I tugged at mum's purse strings to let me have a black Harrington jacket from Castle Market with tartan lining inside - a snip at £5.99.

The Specials were signed to their own label that of 2-Tone Records and very soon The Selecter, Madness and all female combo The Bodysnatchers all released debut singles on the label. On hearing the new ska sound my dad would kiss his teeth and say "dis na skarrr" in that unmistakable disapproving West Indian accent of his, staying loyal to the original sound.

Boxing Day 1979 is the day the red half of Sheffield would rather forget , trouble is the blue half won't let 'em.

On our return to school after father Christmas had done his bit for world peace, the hot topic of conversation between followers of Sheffield United and Sheffield Wednesday was the Owls humiliation of the Blades at Hillsborough.

For weeks after the result the arguments would continue as the Blades boys did everything in their power to convince the non-believers that the 4-0 result in Sheffield Wednesday's favour was a one off, a fluke.

It was decided that if the Blades wanted to settle the score so badly, a match between the blue half of our year and the red half would be organised to take place in the school yard of an evening that suited both parties. (High noon in shorts).

The Blades wasted no time in putting a team together while the Owls struggled for numbers even though they only needed six. It was at this point that the blues turned to Pele (that's me remember) for help and to don a blue and white shirt to help their cause.

Now it's probably the biggest secret on the Wybourn, well not anymore! That I was and still am a massive Leeds United follower yeah I know, Dirty Dirty Leeds. Only a handful of people knew this including my best friend at number 24, but if I had to choose between blue or red, it would definitely be blue every time no question, why? Because I've always found the reds to be arrogant and full of themselves - always have done.

The whole Dirty Dirty Leeds thing came about because Yorkshire Television always used to screen Leeds United highlights on the big match on a Sunday afternoon, and it's there I fell for the men in white, Yorkshire's Real Madrid.

Bremner, Giles, Charlton and Lorimer had long hung up their boots but it was the new generation of mighty whites that had me glued to the TV set, Arthur Graham, Ray Hankin, Terry Connor and Brian Flynn, the new heroes of the hour.

On the evening of the game I was made sub, giving way to someone who actually followed the blues which was fair enough as far as I was concerned, it also came as a bit of a blessing in disguise because by half time Wednesday were actually four goals down with no reply.

There was a huge amount of noise that game because half the school had stayed behind to watch, and believe me it was a real spectacle as both teams in their respective colours went at it from the off in the name of pride.

Even the drivers of the 56 bus kept slowing down on Manor Oaks Road to catch a glimpse what was going on, I also reckon that there were quite a few outsiders that came in through the gates to watch events unfold.

So with the score at 4-0, I was brought on to put the frighteners on the rampant blades, and I almost did it becoming an instant hero and honorary blue nose in the process.

In our first attack of the second half, the ball was slid in front of me a little too far if I'm honest but my long leg met the ball to slide it into the net 4-1. After a couple of minutes more of mounting pressure I slammed home number two and couldn't resist running up to the blades fans who were also pals of mine and giving them the clenched fist sign to their faces which took on worried looks as to where their big advantage was disappearing to.

The Blades seemed to regain their composure after the second went in and from then on in I was shackled for the rest of the game, United went on to bag another two putting the game and Wednesday to bed. With the score at 6-2 it was game over and even though the score line suggests a right hammering that couldn't be further from the truth, if you were there or even played you'll know that it was real edge of the seat stuff from start to finish.

23 years later my performance in that game was recounted in the best man's speech at my wedding and the service took place at, wait for it... downtown Bramall Lane.

During the spring of '80 the fourth year pupils started going on mini excursions to a place called Mayfield, I think it was called that I can't be 100% sure I've got that right, but I'm sure someone will remember.

Each class would take it in turns to venture out there for the day, a sort of field trip if you like, a lesson on the great outdoors, we'd board a coach that was fitted with desks so we could work while we travelled (didn't miss a trick did they!)

A classroom was designated to us in an old Victorian school house that was still being used to educate the local farmers kids who I swear were still using ink pots and feathers to write with, then we'd venture out into the surrounding wilderness collecting cones, acorns and all manner of weird and wonderful stuff. The items were bagged up and then taken back to the classroom so we could talk and write about what we had found.

Now we'd heard from the other class that had been there the week before that the local lads liked nothing more than to challenge their city rivals to a game of football after dinner - and the reports coming back was that they were a little tasty. So having finished our dinner the challenge came via messenger it was game on; Old MacDonald's boys, versus the city kids in the top field - tractors for goalposts.

I have no recollection of how the first game between the two sides went, but what I do know is that we made a lot of friends out there wherever it was, and we were the class they most looked forward to seeing. The local lads couldn't get enough of the girls in our class either, and sometimes I'd have six or seven local girls wanting to touch me and my afro, what I wouldn't give for something similar like that happening to me today.

So with the summer holidays on the horizon it's time for the last roll call, a coming of age has arrived and here is a list of my classmates of whom I'm proud to call true friends. And if I've left anyone out I apologise, hope your well and good luck.

Paula Fairhurst, Darren Oxley, Christine Cheetham, Mick Pickersgil, Katherine Whitaker, Alan Adams, Mandy Beale, Joseph Betts Jr, Avis Clarke, Lee Fisher, Denise Brown, Tony Mannion, Lisa Parker, Paul Norfolk, Christine Rhodes, Craig Frankish, Corrina Hudson, Brian Sanderson, Jenifer Tooze, Mark Ashton, George Warriss Samantha Sutherland and Carl Taylor.

Julian Antonio McKenzie being cradled by his mum on the day of his christening whilst the family were still living in Page Hall

A stickler for style - Julian's dad

Julian's mum (left) and friend

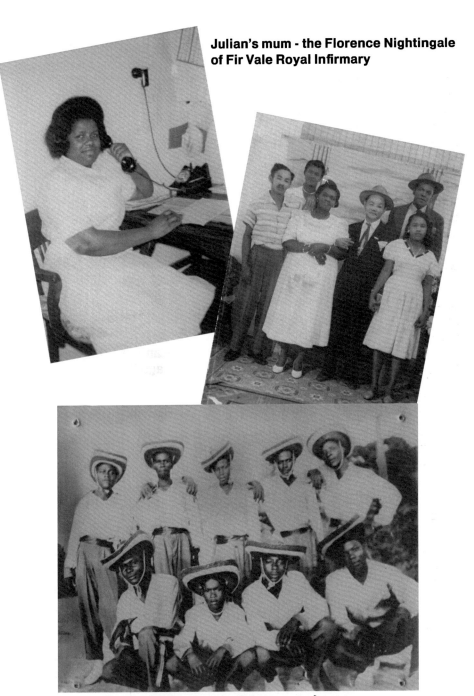

Julian's mum - the Florence Nightingale of Fir Vale Royal Infirmary

Julian's dad (front row, first from left) in his native Dominica as a youngster

Julian (centre), his sister (right) and friend in Millhouses Park

Julian's dad's South Yorkshire
Transport id card

Julian's mum in the 1970s

The Wybourn estate

The streets in the sky of Park Hill - the sprawling inner city council estate set a stone's throw away from Hyde Park where the McKenzie's lived before their move to the Wybourn

Fitzalan Square's Classic Cinema

Sheaf Valley Baths

Celebrating the Silver Jubilee in Sheffield

A rainy day looking up High Street

Wybourn kids on a hot summer's day in the seventies

Kids on the Wybourn in the early seventies

Terry Coleman in recent years - a true friend for life

My lifelong friend Gavin at 9-years old

Terry Hall of The Specials

Hurlfield Here I Come Part 1

"Flippin' 'eck Tucker"..! One of my all-time favourite catchphrases from one of my all-time favourite kids TV shows, and very soon without word or warning I'd have something very much in common with Tucker Jenkins and the rest of the boys and girls at Grange Hill Comprehensive School.

Now your mind's probably doing overtime with this one because those of you who are in the know will remember I never ever crossed the threshold of Hurlfield Comprehensive school, not even close enough to spit.

There is a very good reason for that, well two actually, my mum and dad.

Hurlfield School had a fearsome reputation in the late '70s early '80s. It was widely known that education was made to stand outside in the corridors along with the juvenile delinquents hell bent on taking the rocky road to self-destruction. In short it was advisable to give this institution for higher education a very wide birth indeed.

So just before the big six week break came along I was given the earth shattering news that the wheels had been set in motion to send me off to another school, and ,unbeknown to me, my parents had already applied.

To say I was devastated was an understatement, I cried for weeks. I was so looking forward to more high jinks with the Wybourn crew of whom I shared eight years, only for mum to pull the plug on the whole affair.

When word came through that the application had been successful and I had been accepted I couldn't believe it, I had issues with authority, I was easily led, I was also seen as a problem child yet I'd been accepted.

My first thought was that mum must have lied through her teeth to get me in there, or as a parting shot and their last chance to get one over on me, my teachers had given me a glowing report there was no other explanation for it.

The day I accompanied mum for the grand tour of the school and the traditional meet and greet still gives me nightmares today. Mum and I walked up Southend Road to get the number nine bus that ran along Manor Lane to Manor Park, then we hopped on the number 93 for the short trip to Beaumont Road. As we got off the bus and turned the corner, there it was, my new second home - sentenced to four years hard graft at the Earl of Waltheof Secondary Comprehensive School. Approaching Waltheof was a scary experience in itself, the nerves were showing because I didn't know anybody and I was out of my comfort zone, and worst still I was now in enemy territory, The Manor.

38

I don't think mum truly understood the implications for me a Wybourn lad on his jacks in the heart of the Manor, but I did; it meant a good kickin' every other day if word got out that the enemy was amongst them.

All the way through mum had kept her cards close to her chest about Waltheof because she had saved the best till last, as we entered through the gates my eyes nearly popped out of their sockets and rolled across the tarmac because all the children were dressed the same in identical matching uniform. The change of direction in schooling I was coming to terms with, but this was taking the proverbial.

Grey trousers, white shirt and blazer, and what was that hanging from around their necks? A bloody tie.

The whole layout of Waltheof reminded me of Northern Ireland's Maze Prison which had been in the news over recent months, now here I was about to get a guided tour of its cells.

Induction over with, it was time to collect my uniform from the Co-op on Angel Street in the city centre, I think the whole kit cost mum around £60 to £70, two pairs of grey trousers, three white shirts, blazer with crest and the monstrosity of a tie. The summer holidays gave me a chance to pull myself together and accept the inevitable, but deep down I was distraught and inconsolable, I tried in vain to block things out with endless games of football.

We started playing other groups of lads from different streets and estates as well as amongst ourselves, one of our favourite ding dongs was against the Dover Court Road boys who played their games in the City Road Cemetery close to the top gates just off Manor Lane. The pitch was on a massive piece of land in the graveyard to the left of the gates as you walked in, and it's there we played out some titanic battles.

Some thirty years on, that piece of land has given way to the ungrateful dead, the poor unfortunates who ran out of time through circumstance, my dad now lays in the exact spot his son played out his childhood dreams.

On my first day at Waltheof I walked to school with a lad I had befriended while still at Wybourn juniors who had just moved onto our estate, and it was a local school rivalry that our paths crossed for the very first time.

Woodthorpe versus Wybourn was always a volatile affair and this game was no exception, it was here the two of us met as opposing players.

The game is best remembered for a number of incidents that happened before, during and after the match.

On arrival at Woodthorpe we ran the gauntlet of being pushed from pillar to post by a hostile crowd baying for blood, the blue Ford Transit mini bus we travelled in taking the full brunt of the juvenile attack.

Before kick-off we revealed our secret weapon via the team sheet, we had a girl in our starting line-up who I have to say was a very good player indeed, our very own Gregory's Girl. You should have seen their faces when she ran onto the pitch, it was a real Kodak camera moment to behold.

We won the game 3-1 which didn't please the natives one little bit, who had earlier ransacked our changing room while we played. There was clothes strewn everywhere, pockets picked, and shoes and trainers shoved down the toilets. This didn't bode well for the return at our place because there was sure to be a welcoming committee on hand ready to dish out any retribution where it was warranted. Nasher Roberts would see to that. Thankfully order was restored in the return game which went without incident, even though we lost 4-2. A couple of weeks after the game I spotted my rival outside the shops round the corner from the Windsor, we nodded to each other then I asked how come he was so far off the beaten track? Turns out he was now a resident of Wybourn living on Boundary Road having moved there with his mum, dad, three brothers and a sister.

So on the way to Waltheof School my new pal and I walked up Southend Road and then out of nowhere the moment I was dreading all summer long. The 656 bus, the St Trinians special, would take all the Wybourn kids and others from neighbouring estates up to Hurlfield (bussin' 'em in) via Whites Lane, Manor Oaks, Boundary Road, up Southend Road, down Manor Lane, before turning onto City Road to Manor Top.

My timing couldn't have been much worse, as the buses met us halfway up Southend, my old school mates gave me what for, taking the piss out of the uniform, throwing sandwiches at us through the windows and bombarding us with balloons filled with water not to mention the colourful language. It was all good natured stuff, banter, but it only served to remind me of what I was missing out on, my new mate turned to me and said "friends of yours then"?

I was kind of hoping that I'd be in the same class as someone I knew but when we gathered in the main assembly hall to be placed in class groups my new pal had been called to go elsewhere, leaving me isolated and alone once more.

My new class was 2N2 and headed by the very petite but forthright Miss Potts, one of the nicest teachers I've ever had the pleasure of listening to. I was also joined by a very familiar face.

One of the Wybourn junior boys who was in the same year but different class to me and resided on Maltravers Road, had opted by choice to attend Waltheof. His reasons were straight forward, his big brother had a fearsome reputation at Hurlfield and it was well documented that he was one of Wybourn's biggest hitters, when he walked down the street curtains would close and pets brought in for safety.

He didn't want to be tarred with the same brush, and having the same family name wouldn't have done him any favours at all. So the two of us forged an alliance of sorts, and we later learnt that there were at least six or seven Wybourn ex-pats in the second year so the philosophy became safety in numbers. What we were really doing was circling the wagons ready for our very own little big horn.

The Manor lads and lasses were I have to say spot on with us, making a real mockery of the so called tribal rivalry, and it didn't take us long to gel.

Most of them had come from junior schools relatively close by Pipworth, Acres Hill, Woodthorpe and a few had come from Manor Lane, which was over my neck of the woods.

The cock of the year was in 2N2, which was dead handy when it came on top in the yard as we were great mates within weeks of our meeting. He was one of the nicest kids you could ever wish to meet, a real gentleman, I don't think he really enjoyed the title bestowed upon him but at nearly seven feet tall and built like a brick outhouse, there was no getting away from it. He also doubled up as my main rival for the number one jersey in the school team and I don't mind telling you or him that I was the better keeper out of the two of us, but I always found myself as his number two I just couldn't get that green jersey away from him.

Within the walls of a new school of higher education there were new lessons to master and one of them was French with gentle Ken, Mr Ken Foden. Kenny's French was impeccable as you would imagine with him teaching us the basics, but again like on so many occasions I thought what was the point, most of the class couldn't master English let alone a language that made us sound like a very bad Del Trotter.

Here's a good one, we were taught better Queen's English by a Scotsman! I bet someone in the staffroom was having a right laugh at that one. Mr Christie, aka Agatha, was a nice enough bloke who took the job of polishing our grammar very seriously, trouble was his was terrible; I really do think someone was taking the piss when they assigned him the job.

In my history class I was taught the ways of the world by Miss Leitch.

She was a born fighter and, as far as I was concerned, very passionate about women's issues. I could imagine her chaining herself to many an iron gate in her time, in the name of women's liberation. Emmeline Pankhurst reincarnated if you like, clearly one woman in number ten wasn't enough at that point!

I thought Miss Leitch's dresscode was more Woodstock than classroom, and I imagined that when she entered the staff room she'd refuse the use of a chair preferring to sit on a bean bag instead.

Sport, now you're talking, there were a number of activities to choose from and I fancied something other than football, netball with Miss Atkins was a definite no no, have you seen my legs? Basketball did appeal to me but Mr Ranson was a grumpy old so and so, even though I had the height he found countless flaws in my game, your loss pal. One day I was approached by another games teacher who asked me whether I fancied playing rugby union, I'd watched it many times on *Grandstand* and thought it looked ok, so long as I could avoid being snapped in two, then why not.

I quickly developed a knack of getting hold of the ball and running hell for leather for the try line, the twenty stoner trying to turn me into dog meat was a key factor in my speed I must admit. The only trouble or problem I had with Mr Stafford, the rugby teacher, was that he was a Welshman. Now if you think that is a tad racist please hold you're fire. I love the Welsh, Llandudno remember, but if you're ever going to take rugger lessons from anyone, make sure he or she are anything but Welsh.

Mr Stafford was passionate about the game, he lived and breathed it twenty four seven like a proud Welshman should, but sometimes the passion would be too much to bare.

He couldn't go one training session without saying "ahhh JPRRRRR wouldn't do it like that" or "Garethhhhhh wouldn't do it like that" the Welsh rugby legends names of yesteryear were bounded about every session. JPR Williams and Gareth Edwards ruined my blossoming rugby career.

I did manage to appear in one game against a very talented Ashleigh School, and almost went close to scoring a couple of tries for us but we were soundly beaten, it was a good effort though and I'm almost positive JPRRRRR would have approved.

Religious Education or RE never really sat well with me, I'm a believer no question, but I reckon there's a right time and a right place to bust someone's eardrums with your beliefs. Our teacher was fragile, timid, and very shy his name escapes me but I'm sure there are quite a few of you with your hands up with the correct answer. He must have missed his vocation in life as a fully-fledged preacher because he was the best in his field, but he was all so easy to wind up and we got it off to a fine art.

Like in most lessons the last thing you want to do is pen push for an hour, so each one of his sessions we'd take it in turns to ask the question does God really exist? It was always important to take cover after that, talk about a red hanky and bull he'd be off on one about the importance of Christ our Saviour for the remainder of the lesson, which suited us down to the ground. I don't think he ever cottoned on to what we were doing to him, let's just say each time he never had any marking to do.

Maths was just one of the most bizarre and dangerous lessons I'd ever taken, it was also the first time I was introduced to geometry and algebra, like what was wrong with two plus two?

That lesson was overseen by a man who was a dab hand with a blackboard rubber who would regularly take aim then fire his missile across the room hitting you smack in the middle of the forehead wooden side up every time. The crime? Not paying enough attention. He also would rap your knuckles with a metal rule accompanied by the word's "naughty naughty".

Smart tweed jacket or not, the man was ruthless.

Biology was a definite non-starter, even though Mrs Alliss was as sweet and charming as the name suggested.

Mr Goodrum was ok, sort of, but his metalwork lessons left me rather non plussed. Bending metal one way one lesson, then bending it back the other, bravo Goodrum who could ever accuse you of not fulfilling your teaching obligations. Art surprised me because I was kind of good at it, I was always doodling at home so this was a natural progression. One of my favourite pieces was the Walt Jabsco figure that adorned my favourite record label at the time that of 2-Tone, a man in a black suit, dark shades, white shirt, black tie, pork pie hat, white socks and loafers, I could draw that in my sleep.

My art teacher wasn't impressed though, she never seemed interested in what I had to offer her, leading to many a confrontation, Bossy Bostwick was a real thorn in my backside and I'm almost certain she felt the same way about me, love hate didn't even come close.

My art was good and she knew it, she just wished it wasn't me producing the work, how bad was that?

I think during the course of the year she got married or re-married because she was now known as Mrs Wainwright and requested we address her as such, but I couldn't resist the wind up sticking my hand up for attention and calling out for Miss Bostwick earning me several daggers in the back. When I dropped out of her lesson after a year of verbal sparring I told her where to go, I do hope Bossy Bostwick found somewhere to shove her paint brushes and easel!

What do you get if you cross twenty or so hyper active twelve year olds and half a ton of sausage and minced meat? Answer, absolute carnage that's what, absolute carnage.

This must go down as one of those legendary moments in school life that should always be remembered, ok it's for all the wrong reasons granted, but it's incidents like these that make childhood memories such a joy to relive.

In our Home Economics lesson, cooking to the working classes, we were given the opportunity to try our hand at making a Shepherd's Pie, a seemingly straight forward task wouldn't you agree? Now I'm not quite sure whether it was with Miss Potts or some other poor unfortunate disciplinarian but whoever it was that day, they wouldn't be forgetting their ordeal in a hurry either.

Having made numerous mouth-watering pies and bunging them in at gas mark anything goes, it was decided that we should clean up the place, but what to do with all the sausage and mincemeat that was left over. Thinking caps on, one lad took a lump of the stuff, rolled it into a ball and then launched it across the room hitting one poor girl in her ever developing chest, bulls eye.

The worst thing she could have done after that was counter attack with a piece as big as a human heart, only the intended target was missed altogether hitting some other poor sap minding his own business. To cut a long story short the whole episode turned into a cowboy saloon room brawl, starting off with two people then spiralling into a free for all, even the goody two shoes kids lined up for a slice of the action.

There was meat on the ceiling, on the windows, on the floor, on the walls, on clothes and in hair, and it didn't stop there either. Any passers-by within range were showered with huge chunks of meat as the melee escalated through the open windows. The end result was that each and everyone of us were placed on daily report, the good guys were off it within days of the sentence being passed down, me I went on to destroy a couple of sturdy trees before I was taken off. Deputy head Marshall had never entertained so many bodies in his woodchip covered office.

This was only the first three months of my tenure at Waltheof, and the upshot of it all was I had some serious knuckling down to do. What did I have in common with the Kit Kat machines dotted around the school? I'll tell you, I was always standing outside in the corridors with them.

Wybourn 'o' Wybourn (very short homage)

Never judge a book by its cover, that's what they all say isn't it?
The estate has had its fair share of bad press coverage down the years, and rightly so in some cases, but for an accurate portrayal of a place and its people, you have to meet and understand their way of life.
Most Wybourners would give you their right arm if they had to, they may not have been its original owner, but you know where I'm coming from don't you.
A community that doesn't use fancy window dressing to get itself noticed, simply because what you see is what you get, a down to earth band of people like you and me doing the best they can in a society that can't wait to drop it on them from the greatest of heights.
For so long associated as a breeding ground for ruthless thugs and master criminals, today's Wybourn estate deserves its fair share of the good column inches that are regularly afforded to so many of its well-heeled city rivals.
Wybourn 'o' Wybourn, you'll always do for me!

(told ya)

Hurlfield Here I Come   Part 2

Life on the top end of Wybourn (the posh bit) was good, I couldn't think of anywhere else I'd rather be, nowhere.

52 Southend Road was also home to the best unofficial Two-Tone fan club in Sheffield, well at least I thought so anyway. Three weeks in the making, countless press cuttings, posters, and a multitude of drawing pins later, it was ready to open its bedroom doors in the late summer of 1980. As far as the Shrines went I'd have challenged anyone to top the mass collection of black 'n' white memorabilia and art work I'd accumulated in just over the last year, it was British ska's central headquarters.

One of my most prized possessions was a huge poster of Pauline Black in full musical flow, it was awesome. That same poster was later replaced some years down the line by a little known model by the name of Samantha Fox, sorry Pauline but she did get them out!

Waltheof 'o' Waltheof, you've got no chance of any homage being paid here, I was still trying to get out of the place; just what did I have to do to rid myself of its hold over me and get early release, burn the place down? Whoops, have I just become a suspect?

It didn't take me long to find myself in more hot water. I was wandering through the school yard one day when I was approached by five fourth year pupils hell bent on bovver. Now in my top blazer pocket I had a red and silver Parker Pen, the type that would only use ink cartridges, the Rolls Royce of Parker Pens a gift from mum that set me out from the Reliant Robin Bic Biro crowd.

Anyway, one of the lads took hold of my pen, took the top off, and dropped it nib first onto the floor, job done. As he and his sidekicks walked away the red mist enveloped me as I launched into the ringleader with a flurry of blows to his empty head. I knew the Sheaf Valley thing would come in handy one day because my blows resembled that of someone swimming the English Channel. To give him his due, empty head put up a good fight but as time wore on he was on his last legs, as we grappled each other to the floor that's when his knight in shining armour in the form of a teacher rode to his rescue and broke up the last dance. As we both rose from the floor the teacher would have been blind not to notice the difference in size between us which made me look like the one who had been dishing it out. What he didn't see was that empty head's mates had done a runner when the shit hit the fan. Explanation over with I was given

46

the benefit of the doubt and sent on my merry way, and the pen, well, that was given a quick burial at sea via the toilet chain.

If my sparring partner that day is reading this I'd like a new pen, same make, same model, same year... Good luck with that!

At 12-years-old I'd come to a major decision in my life, it wasn't an easy one for me to make but it had to be done all the same. It was high time I knocked *Finger Bobs* on the head and started watching something a little less childish instead. In its place came the *Red Hand Gang, Rentaghost, Magpie* and *Tiswas*, ITV's mayhem infested Saturday morning show. By now I had let go of mummy's hand and started to venture out further afield with the lads of an evening, the Windsor wall was still out of bounds for us youngsters because of the strict rites of passage policy the wall had for many a year before us.

It meant we were not allowed to hang tough with the older lads until it was time for them to move on with the onset of cars, clubs and girls; wheels, beer and legs.

So what we did to relieve the boring bits in our lives was to go on two pence bus rides all over Sheffield and seeing where the journey would take us.

My dad had a transport book hidden away in an old kitchen drawer and I used to sneak it out of the house so that we could plot our night on the buses. Each journey's end we'd get off at the terminus and then hop back on again, it was a great way of meeting different people, especially the girls. It also provided much needed warmth from the cold during the harsh winter nights.

It was always important to take the back seat then hold your own throughout the journey - "take the back seat take the back seat" was a familiar tune for many a lads gang in the eighties.

On one particular bus ride we were close to tears when we bit off more than we could chew on the number eight circular that took us all over the shop, it just wouldn't stop.

One of the lads swore he saw a sign for Manchester along the way. The number eight and number nine were legendary bus routes that did the full monty guided tour of Sheffield: Hillsborough, Page Hall, Southey Green, Pitsmoor, Abbeydale, Manor Park, Attercliffe, Tinsley, Arbourthorne, you name it, it went there.

I used to laugh my bollocks off when we went through Pitsmoor because the rest of the lads used to crouch down on the floor until the coast was clear and we'd ridden through it.

They just didn't trust the power of having a black member in the gang as a get out of jail card, Bounty bar that's what they used to call me, brown on the outside white on the inside.

The Windsor Hotel was the Mecca for most of the local big hitters in the area who liked nothing more than to relax, have a drink, a fag and a fight.

I had one of the best ringside seats on a Friday and Saturday night and all from the comfort of my bedroom window, as the Windsor courtyard would turn itself into Madison Square Garden hosting the latest heavyweight bout.

If you thought the bell that rang at the end of another heavy drinking session was time, then think again it usually meant round one.

Any differences people had during the night were settled with a good old fashioned toe to toe punch up, last man standing and woman, no guns, no knives like today's idiots, just an old traditional fist fight.

Who bought the last round or who didn't; women or the turn of a dodgy card that hadn't been seen all night would kick things of big time, and back in the day the police were really reluctant to arrive on scene at the Windsor for fear of getting a right good hammering themselves.

Don't you just hate it when people tell you they were the first person to do this of the first person to do that, the first to buy that or the first to buy this, question, how the hell do they know? Well I'm not about to buck the trend here, because I'm about to tell you how I became the only kid in Sheffield and the whole of the United Kingdom to own a pair of monkey shoes (not boots) but shoes.

Once again let's be clear on this, shoes, not the boots that were as common as dog turds in a park, shoes. And how do I know this self-proclaimed fact I here you say? Well that's easy my friends because they didn't bloody exist.

If you remember I got my monkey boots as a gift from mum a few months before Waltheof welcomed me with open arms and mum had deemed them good enough to wear to school.

She'd already forked out a king's ransom on the prison garb from the Co-op and a new pair of shoes would have broken the bank, so it was decided my boots would be my school shoes by day and my bovver boots by night, sorted or so we thought.

During one lesson we were all sat doing our work with the teacher pacing up and down each row of desks as they did, when he suddenly hit the brakes and did an emergency stop at my feet. He looked at my boots and proclaimed they were not regulation footwear in keeping with the schools strict dress code policy, in English that meant "can't wear those".

Five minutes later I found myself up before the headmaster Mr Alan (I just haven't got a clue what to do) Bardgit, the schools new head who had taken over the reins from Mr Postlethwaite just before I arrived.

Bardgit himself was a new recruit like me and was flexing his muscles in a show of who's boss, the king is dead, long live the king. After a short speech

I was given a two week suspension to take immediate effect and a change of footwear would secure my return.

When I got home earlier than usual and told mum why she blew her top, hell have no fury like a Jamaican woman vexed believe me. When dad arrived, he took in the news, had his tea, then kissed his teeth, food first problems later! The next few days, mum and dad put their collective heads together on how best to solve the mini crisis, but both were adamant there would be no new purchases of shoes. I could see Hurlfield on the horizon once again back in the bosom of my Wybourn buddies, it was only a matter of time, wasn't it?

My dad was, it has to be said, a very good amateur cobbler and would mend peoples shoes mainly friends in his spare time with the aid of two wooden block moulds in the shape of feet which would help him to do the work on the shoes with relative ease. One evening he took hold of my bovver boots, stared at them for a while then with a smirk set to work on them, but what was he going to do? I looked at mum who in turn looked at me, as we didn't have a clue what was about to happen.

Dad put the wooden blocks into the boots and secured the blocks tight inside, then he took out his razor sharp leather cutting knife and proceeded to slice the top half of the boots that covered the balls of my ankles.

I was in floods of tears at this point because he'd just murdered my boots in cold blood.

After a lot of banging, hammering, cutting and stitching, I was presented with a new pair of shoes, and thus they were born, my monkey shoes. If anyone knew how to beat the system it was the old man. So a week after the suspension was passed, I returned to school in my new form of boots, my trousers covered most of my shoes so you couldn't see the drastic change that had taken place.

When I marched into school everyone thought I was the biggest rebel since James Dean, even the tough nuts in smokers' corner couldn't believe the gall of the cheeky black kid taking on the school head on. They all thought I was about to give Waltheof School the rods - come and get me style.

At registration a lot of fuss was made over me and I'd like to think my new classmates actually missed me, but Miss Potts soon put a stop to the welcoming committee. She took one look at me, then my feet and nearly passed out on the spot thinking I'd defied the law of the land. It was time to reveal the truth. So I lifted my trouser legs and showed the class and the rest of the world my newly acquired fashion statement. The whole place erupted with laughter at the sight of the decapitated footwear and it didn't stop for a good five minutes after that, I felt humiliated and embarrassed at the same time.

It was only the beginning of my woes because it didn't take long for the school jungle drums to pick up the beat in broadcasting the hilarious events that had unfolded in 2N2.

During break times and dinner, I was subjected to cruel taunts and jokes about what was on my feet, the rubber neckers were out in full force that day.

Flicking through the "currant bun" one evening I noticed on ITV a *World In Action* special to be aired that very evening was about to start. *World In Action* was a popular current affairs programme in the eighties, not the sort of viewing you'd associate with a 12 -year-old kid, but this particular episode looked very interesting indeed.

The programme highlighted the plight of eight unemployed teenagers from Birmingham trying to live life as best they could on the dole. Frustrated with their efforts they decided to form a band, thus drawing the dole in the day and practicing as a band at night. The programme charted their success at securing a record deal with a relatively unknown record label, and the release of their debut album very aptly titled, 'Signing Off'.

UB40 was the first ever gig I attended at the Sheffield City Hall in the spring of '81, and I had become an avid fan since the World In Action special had aired. The City Hall wowed me the moment I set foot in the place and my only thought was that the Beatles played here. The venue was only half full that night but that didn't matter to the one thousand or so diehards in the audience who were treated to a British reggae and dub extravaganza.

Forty had just released second album, 'Present Arms', establishing themselves as one of the best acts of the year.

I went to the gig on my own, but there were quite a few Wybourn faces in the crowd that night so I felt safe in the knowledge I wasn't truly alone. The 'Present Arms' album was never off the turntable at home, and even mum who was from the reggae capital of Jamaica, couldn't fail to be impressed at the sounds coming out of the speakers.

Break time, and everyone who was anyone rushed over to the sports notice board to see who had made the school team to face Beaver Hill Comprehensive. I was 100% confident in my ability as a good shot stopper, and the rightful owner of the number one green jersey that was up for grabs, there was no contest.

But it was something I said in my first weeks at Waltheof that would ultimately close the lid on my school team football career, and a grudge that would last till the day I left the building for good. Gutted isn't the correct word I'd use when I saw my name wasn't on the team sheet that afternoon, I felt sick and twisted with rage, my mate and cock of the year had made the number one position his own.

Right there and then I felt like nutting him on the bridge of his nose Wybourn style, but who was I kidding, he'd have turned me into some form of brown slush no questions asked.

There was a flicker of hope though because I was chosen to play in the B team to play Acres Hill on the same morning, so all was not lost. On a bright Saturday morning I played a blinder against the school from across the way, but overall we were out-classed and out-played by a very good team. My defence that morning went AWOL throughout the 90 minutes, still wrapped up in their six million dollar man duvets no doubt, it was like the Alamo. The final score was 5-1 in their favour and I was disappointed I'd conceded so many. After the game the referee who just happened to be a teacher at Acres Hill, ran up to congratulate me on my display. At first I thought Mr Lovett was taking the piss, but he was genuine in his praise explaining that they should have run up a cricket score but for me, nice words I thought "thank you".

As we all approached the changing rooms I heard someone call out my name. As I turned around I saw Mr Ellis the games supremo calling me over, what the hell did Stumpy want?

It turned out my pal had done his back during the A team game with Beaver Hill, and with the game poised at 4-4 and ten minutes left they needed cover to see out the game. What I really felt like doing was giving Stumpy the brown rods but thought better of it and answered their SOS. It was like the Alamo all over again, I was amazed the hill stalled at four. The A team were all over the shop, headless chickens sprang to mind. I was finally beaten by a deflected shot that left me stranded like Mr Crusoe, there was nothing I could do to stop the ball sailing in. So in the space of ten minutes more I was trooping off the field of play a loser for the second time, the A team lads were great with me acknowledging there was nothing I could do, besides the damage had already been done well before I arrived on the scene.

Mr Ellis and I had history, we were at loggerheads the day I turned up at one of my first games lessons and enquired whether he was really my games teacher, because at the time I thought he was a little on the large size to be just that.

From that moment on I never really recovered from that slip of the tongue and seemed to pay for it for the next four years of my tenure at Waltheof.

One day Mr Ellis received a phone call from Acres Hill, and Mr Lovett was on the other end of the line; it transpired they had lost their goalkeeper just before a huge match and Mr Lovett was enquiring whether he could borrow a keeper from his school neighbours.

Legend has it Ellis went through his list of names before being cut off in his prime by Mr Lovett who said he wanted the black kid he'd faced a few weeks earlier in the season.

When he relayed the news to me I bet he took a very deep breath, then counted to ten before approaching me.

What does true love feel like, look like, or even taste like? All those questions and more besides were floating around in my head the moment I clapped eyes on a young Parisian woman who had come to our school on a teaching scholarship from France to learn the ways of her English counterparts.

Angel Briquette (say it in French, it sounds far sexier) changed the way I felt about education, life, and love the day she breezed into our lessons as part of her learning forum; her long black hair and supermodel looks, topped off with plum red lips designed for sensual kissing made me wonder whether she'd taken a wrong turn at Paris fashion week and ended up here, on the Manor.

I'm hoping that out of the twenty of so classmates I had someone will remember her, if not this is going to sound like one boys exaggerated fantasy but it's the truth.

Angel and I got on like an arsonist and a box of matches. I adored her and would do anything to grab her attention in class - all of a sudden two plus two became a huge problem for me knowing full well she'd come over to help me.

I was in love I could feel it, not down there, but in my heart, we made each other laugh and enjoyed each other's company, not just in the classroom but at weekends too.

Angel was 19 and I had just turned 13, but she was childlike with her 19 years and we had so much in common, she lived in student accommodation on Eccesall Road, and on Saturdays I would meet her in Pond Street and we'd drink coffee in the Transport Café, show a girl a good time that's me!

I knew her stay in England wouldn't be a long one, but I decided to put it at the back of my mind until the day arrived; I think I was hoping she'd take me back to Paris with her, and you know what I would have gone, I'm pretty certain about that.

When the day arrived and Angel said goodbye I was lost for words, nothing would come out; I think I tried to tell her that I loved her but the bottle was shot to pieces.

In the end I let Angel go without telling her how I felt, one of the biggest regrets of my life.

A few days after her departure a letter arrived for me through the post, I knew straight away who the sender was as I tore at it like a crazed animal.

I read the letter slowly, carefully, over and over again and in it, right at the end, the words I failed to tell her:

'The Buzzcocks were playing my tune'

Gerald Dankey Broke My Heart

It had to be the biggest crime wave the Wybourn estate had ever seen, in my time anyway. Choppers, Chippers, Tomahawks, Grifters, BMX's, racers, skateboards, Space hoppers and even next door's cat went missing in a spate of thefts that went unnoticed under the cover of darkness. No one knew who, or how, but it wouldn't take long for the good people of Wybourn to turn their attention to the instigator and criminal mastermind behind the snatch and grab raids sweeping the estate, step forward Mr Television himself, and BBC TV royalty, Noel Edmonds Esquire.

Edmonds and his *Swap Shop* Saturday morning road show were due to hit Sheffield's Norfolk Park for a live television broadcast witnessed by the rest of the country.

The excitement swept through the estate and I guess countless others in Sheffield like wild fire and not only that, it also meant Sir Keith Chegwin would be winging his way up north to entertain us with his legendary madcap antics and tomfoolery.

Now I'm guessing that the researchers at the beeb hadn't done their homework properly because had they chosen any other Sheffield park the turn out wouldn't have been so high, but Norfolk Park was central for everyone. Five minutes from the town centre and you were virtually on top of it, so that meant only one thing, most of the nastiest and troublesome estates in Sheffield and their inhabitants would be descending on the place in their droves. Not just respectable families with young children, but the big boys and let's not forget the big girls who loved a good tear up every once in a while with their nearest and dearest cross city rivals. A huge recipe for disaster. The main ingredients that day was as follows:

Shiregreen, Parson Cross, Darnall, Tinsley, Foxhill, Batemoor, Manor, Abourthorne, Low Edges, Wybourn, Park Hill, Walkley, Firth Park, Wharncliffe, Pitsmoor, Shirecliffe, High Green, Hackenthorpe, Wisewood, Frechville, Woodseats and countless others on the map, add a few Rotherham heads give a good stir, leave to simmer, then stand well back.

No need to bring to the boil, the day would take care of everything.

We considered Norfolk Park as Wybourn Territory, just like the British Empire in its heyday we had colonised the park, Sky Edge and parts of the Manor as our own, but this was an invasion even the yanks would have struggled to contain. The *Swap Shop* format was fairly simple, if you wanted to rid yourself of old games, books, toys, and dare I say it bikes, you could do so via a phone call to the Swap Shop studio who in turn would put you in touch with someone who was willing to trade your items for theirs. If anything took your fancy and vice versa, a deal was struck over the phone with Noel as the man in the middle (the broker).

The show was a massive hit that pulled in millions of viewers every Saturday morning, the show also featured special guests and musical artists, some of whom making their career defining TV debuts. I have to be honest in saying I wasn't a huge fan of the show, too much like goody two shoes TV, the chaotic mess that was *Tiswas* was more in keeping with my teenage lifestyle at the time. Armed with goodies, some of them under mum's radar, we trooped off down to the park. The place was choc a bloc with invaders pushing and shoving trying to get the best vantage and viewing spots. We were desperate to get on the TV ourselves and would stand in front of cameras, any cameras, in the hope we'd be beamed back into the nation's living rooms.

After placing our booty in a secret location within the park we took a closer look around the back of the BBC trailers, only to be confronted by a security guard and his very hungry looking, foaming at the mouth companion, 'nice doggy'! Any rich pickings that day were put on hold for the foreseeable future. The whole day was probably a researchers dream, there was none of the expected trouble whatsoever, not even a murmur; it was almost as if a secret pact had been written and signed by the warring factions in the crowds.

We didn't get close enough to do any swapsies, the heaving masses proving to much for us on the day.

After the live broadcast was over and the crowds started to disappear, we offered our services helping the BBC crew dismantle scaffolding and rolling up cables, for a small fee of course, the cash never materialised but we did obtain some *Swap Shop* goodies as a reward and a pat on the head.

Keith Chegwin was as daft as he portrayed himself on the box even when the cameras stopped rolling, the cheeky chappie wouldn't or couldn't stop laughing, at what we didn't have a clue, but we were in awe of the little fella from the moment we met. One of the lads then asked Keith whether we could cadge a lift home with the gear we didn't manage to swap, we were only up the road. In my humble opinion I do believe Cheggars was ready to jump in a spare BBC Land Rover and duly oblige if it were not for several researchers grabbing his keys and ushering him away into the mass of trailers.

Can you imagine turning up on the Windsor wall in a chauffeur driven Land

Rover with Cheggars at the wheel!

I was now a third year inmate at Waltheof, and a brand new term meant a brand new form teacher, and he came in the shape of the ultra-intelligent Mr Blabey in class 3Gp.

Our new classroom was slap in the middle of the canteen so if you were Hank Marvin during the morning the torment of various foods being prepared by the kitchen staff would send you over the edge. Luckily we only had one lesson in there so it wasn't so bad of an ordeal, or was it? Because the lesson we took in that classroom was German, in my opinion the most aggressive language in the world. I just couldn't get to grips with it all, after six or seven months of trying, 'Sieg heil' and 'Heil Hitler' was my only contribution and that was me done. The classroom was pretty basic and rather small with no windows but it did have an air conditioning fan built into the ceiling that would spin 24/7 whatever the weather. We threw all sorts up into that fan in a bid to make it stop. Just kids having a laugh, I guess the temptation was hard to resist. Things included: Screwed up balls of paper, pens, pencils, half eaten sarnies, text books, Mars Bars, and one training bra were launched upwards into the blades, but don't worry too much about the last item because its owner had her feet firmly on the ground when that went up! On Fridays we used to go to the Annexe, a supplementary building in Darnall at the back of Staniforth Road. It was an old school building that housed woodwork and metalwork rooms, an art class, maths class and a fully functional kitchen for home economics (minus the mince) which was strictly off the menu this term. We loved going down there, it was a welcome change from the norm; at break times we'd take on the other class that accompanied us down there to a game of football using a tennis ball because the regulation size football was banned for fear of damaging the ageing windows of the 18th century building . At lunchtime the food was shipped in from Acres Hill, and let me tell you, you've never tasted chips, fish fingers and peas like these in your life, my compliments to the chef, and a Michelin star rating.

Saturday mornings were now reserved for hanging out on the gallery in town just off Dixon Lane or opposite whichever way you looked at it. The long walkway stretched all the way round to the Castle and Sheaf markets. It also provided easy access to Woolworths, British Home Stores and Rebels nightspot along with other small outlets along its balcony; and that's where you would find us between 10am and 2pm slap bang outside Woolworth's second floor entrance.

The spot had the best view of everything that was happening beneath us. You oould see most of Fitzalan Square to the left and the Cannon Pub and the Old

Crown Court building to the right.

We'd stand directly in the middle watching the busy shoppers down below going about their weekend business, sometimes dropping sweets into their shopping bags as they slowly filed past; we didn't always hit the target though, leaving us no option but to leg it from our position until the coast was clear. You could eye up groups of girls sat on the top deck of all the buses that went past and if contact was made and you felt sure you had a tug, you'd race down to Pond St or up High Street to meet them of the bus.

After a couple of hours of target practice and bird pulling on the gallery, it was down Dixon Lane and destination Barrow Boys - a cavern like ale house where the Blades boys used to congregate on a home match day.

Sitting opposite on the kerb, we'd watch as their numbers swelled into a heaving mass of red and white, all of them getting tooled up on Tetley's, Magnet, Stones and whatever else they could throw down their necks before kick-off. Around 2.30pm the place would empty as the hordes, now split into two groups, headed off toward the aircraft hangar that was Pond Street bus depot singing in unison at the tops of their voices.

The other half of the red and white delegation would tail off toward Midland Station, picking off any away day stragglers left behind from the main mob who had probably been police escorted to the lane.

I once watched the united boys run West Ham out of town, scattering the southerners all over Paternoster Row and into the station; they were really on fire that day.

The hammers were no mugs and wreaked havoc in towns and cities the length and breadth of Britain but the infamous ICF were well and truly humbled that day.

New romanticism was all over the show come '81, but I still had black and white blood coursing through my veins from the onset of the two-tone uprising of '79.

But there were rumours abound that all was not well in Skaville. The Specials were on the brink, everyone knew it but chose to ignore the cracks that were being well documented by the music press; I didn't want them to split, no way, I was fearful of a future without them, plus I hadn't seen them live yet, so they couldn't not yet anyway.

My chance came when the band announced they were to play a free concert at the Herringthorpe Valley playing fields in Rotherham for the masses of South Yorkshire, an unofficial farewell if you like, and with a number one single at the top of the pop tree what a way to go, if indeed that was the case.

The day itself was fraught with danger as small pockets of Rotherham skins formed welcoming committees at the bus station, the number 69 from city drawing the most attention as it carried half the population of Sheffielders who were on the beano to their green and pleasant land.

The plan that day was not to ask anyone for directions, otherwise we may as well have worn signs around our neck saying 'out of towners, slap us' so we decided to follow any splinter groups who looked as though they knew where they were going.

Easier said than done, there were punks, teds, mods and even a few new romantics who were probably there to finally see off the spectre of two-tone once and for all, their very own dawning of a new era .

The Specials gave the public and me what they wanted, a rip roaring finale to a brief career, and my instant thought was if they did decide to call it quits then wherever they may wander individually or otherwise, I would follow.

Spoilt for choice that's what I was at this point in time as my mates and friends multiplied tenfold, at home and at school. I never thought I'd get on with the Manor and Darnall crowd, but I was wrong about that on so many levels, they weren't just my classmates anymore, we were family and just like it was at Wybourn Nursery and Junior school, we were growing up together, year in year out.

I'd sometimes head down onto Darnall of an evening to hang out with my school pals outside Darnall libs or on Greenland way, just having a laugh and making a nuisance of ourselves.

Most nights I'd hang out up our end either playing football on Ozzy's field, Manor Lane or hanging on the Windsor wall. Membership now accepted even if it was three years to early. I even made friends with a group of gypsy kids who were living on Stuart the farmer's field on Manor Lane, like I said friend to many, foe to few.

Meanwhile at school I very nearly alienated myself from the regular crowd when I started lusting after one of the smell kids. The smell kids were named so because they didn't half pen and ink, to be fare probably not their fault I blame the parents, but they hummed big time.

One of the girls in the smell group was really pretty and I'd talk to her endlessly, I even caught the number 71 bus with her at home time just to be near her.

The 71 circular would stop directly outside the school going down to Darnall and the Cliffe, while across the road you could catch it going the other way to manor top before turning right on its way down to city road.

My intention would be to get off at City Road squeezing every minute of talk time out of her as I could, unfortunately the smell was so bad I'd call it a day and get off at Manor Top taking in the fresh air at the same time as giving her a loving wave and a flash of the pearly whites.

Another object of my smouldering teenage desire was a young lady in class 2E2 who did it for me for real, trouble was I couldn't get near her, she was a Darnall lass who possessed one of the deadliest left hooks I've ever had the pleasure of being hit with. Every birthday and Christmas I'd buy her chocolates and a card in the hope of hitting first base at least, but no chance she was having none of that, and to think those chocs cost me two quid a pop.

She's probably out there somewhere, a mother superior in a convent in the Swiss Alps, yeah touched by an angel but not by me.

Here we go again, more teenage kicks this time with the girl about 12 or 14 doors down from my house, I didn't have a clue what school she attended but she sure looked the business in green blazer, green skirt, white shirt, and grey tights. On a school morning I used to time my entrance from our yellow front gate to coincide with her walk up Southend Road, she was a walking talking Harmony hairspray advert, as her tresses flowed in every direction. Sometimes my timing was way off the mark and I'd end up walking ahead of her, and on numerous occasions I'd end up waking behind her, though looking back that wasn't exactly the end of the world, if you know what I mean. When I did manage to get it right our paths would cross, she'd smile and say hello and I would then inadvertently wet myself losing control of the whole situation.

And I wasn't the only one of our class whose hormones were dancing around inside them, my mate started seeing a new girl who had just started at school in our year who was a dead ringer for Curt Smith of Tears For Fears fame, right down to the pony tail at the back of her shaven head.

We took the piss nonstop, "when you seeing Curt again" "can you get us tickets for the next gig", all good humoured stuff and what a lovely girl she was too.

Tell me I wasn't the only one who got it horribly wrong when Boy George made his *Top Of The Pops* television debut, tell me it was an easy mistake to make!

Bradley's Records on the top of Fargate was fast becoming my second home, the Mecca for every good record collector worth his or hers salt. You could smell the vinyl cuts as soon as you opened the door.

Rows and rows of chart toppers neatly placed with due care and attention by a loyal staff that took pride in their work; the place was the stuff of legend, compact, neat and welcoming. The stairs leading down to the cassette department were steep, so steep that many a customer must have put in a claim at one time or the other.

I recall buying the new Fun Boy Three LP from Chelsea Girl of all places. If Bradley's didn't have what you were looking for your second port of call would have been big Kev's Roulette Records on the High Street.

Kev was going out with a Wybourn lass at the time and I do believe they're still going strong, he was a top bloke who knew his stuff musically and otherwise. On this occasion Kev must have been clean out of Fun Boy Three because if Roulette couldn't satisfy your needs then it really was last chance saloon at Chelsea Girl who had a record department in their basement.

I always felt I didn't belong when I walked through the doors of Chelsea, well come to think of it I didn't, it was a birds clothes shop after all.

The stairs led you down to a pair of saloon type doors the type you'd see in any cowboy or John Wayne movie, push them to go through and they'd swing shut behind you. It was like a different world down there, very chilled and relaxed with a strange hypnotic smell luring you further inside. The record section was pretty impressive, and not only that there were changing cubicles down there too, so you couldn't really help yourself from turning your attention away from the latest vinyl releases and kopping a look at a half decent, half-dressed dolly bird.

I had no qualms about visiting the town centre on my own now, for me it was that coming of age thing.

Long gone were the days of holding onto mummy's hand tightly as we took in what Redgates at the top of the Moor had to offer, I was independent, flash and oozed confidence. This all culminated in me choosing and buying my own threads, well mum still provided the dough but you know what I mean.

Since the sudden demise of two-tone and the Specials, my look and appearance started to change. Some would argue that two-tone wasn't dead just yet, but in my opinion the whole episode should have been laid to rest when the lads from Coventry closed the door behind them.

I wasn't deliberately trying to change my image, but the '80s seemed to brainwash everyone into thinking they had to, and you know what they say! If you can't beat 'em...

Double breasted shirts, Lee Cooper jeans, and black slip on pointy shoes, no socks, and smile, yes the tide was turning and turning fast.

Harringtons in Castle Market

Redgates

**Bomber
Graham
(left) and
trainer
Brendon
Ingle
(centre)**

Miner's leader Arthur Scargill

**Woolco on
Castle Market**

The Hole In The Road gears up for Christmas

Police on the streets in the Miner's Strike in Sheffield

The Stonehouse

We're Only Making Plans For….

Who could have thought that my mum's Littlewoods and Grattan catalogues, would have supplied me with a rich supply of visual contact with the opposite sex, porno for the true beginner.

The Toxteth and Brixton riots of '81 left me with a feeling of shame and bewilderment, as a young black youth (or 'yoot' as my 'bredrin' would say) I wondered what the public perception of me was. Although I wasn't directly involved in the free for all, it was the black man's struggle against constant police harassment that had sparked the remarkable scenes witnessed all over the country.

Well rest assured the Wybourn Estate could sleep easy in their beds safe in the knowledge that this black yoot wouldn't be turning their cars over on its roof, or throwing milk bottles filled with BP's finest at their front doors.

My second term at Waltheof was drawing to its close and once again the big six week break was beckoning, the next term after that was seen by many as the all-important one. Important because it was the one in which you would be studying your chosen options.

But before the old term was over with, you needed to have settled on what subjects you wanted to take, and what career path you wanted to tread.

I myself had some serious thinking to do, what I really wanted was a career in football, but not on the playing side of things I was nowhere near good enough for that, but the journalistic side of the game really excited me.

Before I could achieve that goal (pardon the pun) it would take some major classroom surgery on my part to be ever taken seriously.

Just as predicted nobody believed I had the attention span to pursue a career in journalism, in fact nobody believed I had the attention span for anything.

In the end I got my own way and chose the subjects I needed to make the natural progression to roving football reporter, some of which made me wonder why they were so important to the cause.

I used to cut the pictures of football reports from the major national newspapers, place them on plain A4 paper and write my own rendition of the previous day or nights action. Ace football commentator John Motson used to do a similar thing when he set out on the long journey to becoming the household name he is today, only he used to turn the sound down on key games, and commentate over the action, there's method in our madness wouldn't you say?

64

In the run up to the hols, to mine and everyone else's surprise, I landed a job at the school tuck shop (me, a Wybourn lad and petty cash! Surely not). It was part of the schools trust initiative and I revelled in the roll as a young adult with added responsibilities.

But it didn't take long for me to turn into Waltheof's modern day version of Robin Hood, stealing from the rich (the school) to give to the poor (my mates). In the days when a Mars Bar cost 15p, I'd take a fifty pence piece and give change for a pound, it was so easy, there were at least eight other kids behind the counter and the huge surge of people wanting to be served and the chaos that ensued made it a doddle to diddle the books.

We had no till, just an empty cardboard box with some lose change the float, and away we went.

Everyone who I knew well were walking around the school with bulging pockets of change every day, and the surprising thing about it all was no one had a clue as to what was going on. At cashing up time according to the mathematical boffins everything tallied up, tell you what I'd have sacked every member of the maths department on the spot.

I was introduced to cross country running during our games lessons and I have to say I loved it, we used to run round the school twice passing the science block, the all-weather pitches, and the Asian block of classrooms that catered for the Indian and Pakistani pupils who would often take different lessons from us.

Some of the Asian kids I'd already befriended and would try to impress them by speaking their language of sorts, very badly indeed. My dad could speak Urdu, so I would copy what I heard him say, looking back maybe I should have asked him what it all meant, at least I didn't offend anyone, no punches were thrown in my general direction. Anyway back to the cross country I loved it and would do really well with my times and finishing position, a creditable third wasn't exactly a failure was it? Top spot would always go to my pal and arch rival for that number one spot in the school team, I just couldn't beat him, once again upstaged by him for the umpteenth time, oh well mate you got the sporting prowess, and I got stuck with the looks. I was invited to represent the school at a cross country event that was taking place at Silverdale School and rumour had it that several key members of the Hallamshire Harriers were in the small crowd. Putting on that number before the start made me feel ten feet tall and very important, if only the lads could see me now!

All the competitors gathered at the start, there must have been two hundred plus all pushing and jostling for position when the flag went down we shot off like hares at the dog track all clustered together until the expected breakaway. As we hit the first hurdle a small group in front of me fell arse over tit onto the path we were following leading to a domino effect that left me and countless others nursing serious injury to ankles, knees and hands.

My race was over, my knee was split a deep wound had appeared where my knee cap used to be, I was in tears through the sheer pain of my fall, and not only that several runners had trampled over my body with spikes.

I'll never forget my brief brush with cross country super stardom nor shall I forget the race at Silverdale School, the huge scar on my left leg won't ever let it lie.

Evenings on my patch, the promised land, were always a good laugh; there was always someone to take the rise out of or something interesting to do.

Quite often we'd hang out on the vent on Sky Edge which was part of a small old peoples' home opposite Viney's on Manor Lane. The vent was a huge ventilation window that would blow warm air from the basement kitchen, and it's there you would find us sat in a circle on blue milk crates telling stories and fantasising about dream conquests with even dreamier girls.

When we hung out on the Windsor wall, nearly always we'd be joined by two community support workers who would drop by for a chat and generally keep an eye on us, in short they were there to keep us out of trouble.

With a success rate of 0% out of 100 you could say they failed miserably, but Mick and Ashley were great lads and would organise events and trips out during the holidays.

They respected us as young adults with a lot of time on our hands and in return we respected them as older adults with nothing better to do with their time, (only joking boys). Thank you.

Football gamesmanship took on a whole new dimension when we, the lads, were joined by four brothers from one of the roughest, toughest families on Southend Road. Every evening we'd all gather on St Oswalds playing fields, elect two captains, and they in turn would choose the players worthy of their choice. Thankfully I was never last pick, it was a hard thing to live down in our inner circle.

The brothers were always split two per team, and believe me when I tell you they were out for blood, not ours, but sibling blood, they absolutely loathed each other on the football pitch. The eldest was a really nice guy and would take great pleasure in dishing it out to his younger bros, the youngest was a real head case who used to play in his steel toe capped pit boots. Going into every tackle like a (mad) man possessed, a 50/50 ball became 100% his as he steamed in with the bright sunshine glaring off the steel toe caps. We had some great games and times, all of us playing till we couldn't run anymore and were fit to drop. But that was only until the process was repeated again the following night and the night after that.

World Cup year was here again, and this time more than any other time England were going to get it right, that's according to Ron Greenwood's twenty-two man squad who had hit the pop charts with the catchy ditty, boasting of how the World Cup was theirs for the taking.

The tabloid press were still putting a downer on their chances; something that will never change I'm afraid, they couldn't wait to mention the boys of '66.

Even today, nearly 50 years on, today's heroes are still slapped in the face with Ramsey, Moore and Geoff Hurst who are annoyingly wheeled out every time England go for crowning glory.

As well as games of footy we enjoyed playing British bulldog and one of my personal favourites, back hopping. The art of back hopping was simple, don't get caught. We started at the top of Southend and would jump fences and walls all the way down to the bottom of the railings surrounding St Oswalds School. There were plenty of pitfalls along the way like ponds, dogs, and brick walls with glass embedded into the top of the wall which was legal back then.

To combat the glass problem I used to borrow my Dad's thick bus driving gloves which could withstand anything, even the heat from a nuclear bomb.

On Sundays we'd go up to Millhouses and the lido with our towels rolled up under our arms; there were a number of buses that went up there, the 24, 17 and number 4 all dropped you off on the doorstep. Once inside we'd strip off, throw our clothes in any empty space then all jump in making a huge splash much to the annoyance of the other revellers in the pool.

'Oh Mr Ambassador, you are spoiling us'! BBC1, BBC2, ITV and now Channel 4. A mind blowing choice of entertainment at our fingertips, well it was five really because we as a family a couple of years previously had struck gold when we found Tyne Tees when trying to retune the tele.

Four was being championed as the modern day television phenomenon although you wouldn't have thought it with the channel's first offering to open up proceedings.

The now iconic *Countdown* with that bloke off *Calendar* news, Richard Whiteley, got the ball rolling, and thankfully things could only and did get better.

The arrival of brand new Liverpudlian soap, *Brookside*, and my all time favourite music show, *The Tube*, hosted by ex-Squeeze keyboard wizard Jools Holland, and the purring sex kitten that was Paula Yates, made Channel Four as popular as its older well established TV rivals.

Art was back on the menu this new term, my third, and having kicked bossy

Bostwick into touch I teamed up with the ultra-cool and trendy Mr Smith. Smith was a dead ringer for a post Beatles Ringo Starr, never seen without his trademark brown box leather Jacket, Hush Puppy loafers and baggy cords, Smith was a really relaxed, chilled out and far out dude maaan!

There were four different languages to choose from this option year, but I knocked all of them on the head, French, German, Spanish and everyone's favourite BAD…

I took on maths at B level with whispering Mr Harris, another one of those laid back dudes who definitely wouldn't have remembered the '60s, and you know what they say, if you do, you weren't really there at all.

My other key subjects under the spotlight were geography with Mr Tiffin, English and English lit, and I do believe social and economic studies were taken with man mountain Mr Evans.

To be or not to be, that was the question, biology or chemistry? I didn't want to do any of them, but, I had no choice in the matter (so they said) it was one or the other, biology with Mr Mellor versus chemistry with Miss Schemeld. In the end I opted for chemistry (if only I could go back in time!) Miss Schemeld and I, in my opinion, seem to share a bit of a love hate relationship. She took the love part of things being a teacher and all, and I took up the slack with the hate. That isn't entirely true to be honest because I was quite fond of her, she made me laugh without even trying. She, I presume, thought wearing a white butcher's coat and Deirdre Barlow-style glasses on a chain made her a top scientific boffin.

Like all good school rivalries ours was quite intense, more verbal sparring than anything else and just like TV's *Grange Hill* our main rivals and theirs shared the same name, Brook.

Ok I know it was Brookdale in the kids drama. But Brookies like in Grange Hill got up everyone's noses.

Their main claim to fame was that Tom Bailey of Thompson Twins fame used to teach there, and boy have they dined out on that one ever since.

The Brookies talked a good fight but when it came to pistols at dawn they were always a no show. I lost count of how many times Waltheof crossed Prince of Wales Road for a toe to toe in Bowden Woods, but the only thing creeping around when we got there was the wildlife.

Home was a happy one. We didn't really want for anything and with a sackful of mates between us, what more could we ask for? A new family of Irish origin moved in at number 32 on the very end of the keyhole and it didn't take long for the boys out of the family to join forces with the other kids whose ages were now ranging from 12 to 18.

Dave, John and Pamela joined our member's only club of John, Debbie, Lee, Lisa, Donna, Allsion, Jane Ian, Lisa, Paul, Lisa Karen, Darren, Dawn, Paul, Claire, yours truly and sister Tracey and our new neighbours Tina, Lisa (another one) and their petrol head brother Andrew.

My dad was winding things down with the bus driving and who could blame him, he was coming up 30 years behind the wheel, it was now time to relax a little.

Mum had given up on the nursing for a while which culminated in her landing a job at Bassetts of Hillsborough on the nightshift. We always knew when she was home because there were wine gums, jelly babies, and coconut mushrooms all over the show, I'd never eaten so many babies and mushrooms in my life. Just thinking about them makes me want to throw up, in fact I'm going to have to leave you for a moment while I...

Every so often one of our girl mates would do a spot of babysitting and as soon as her employers were out of sight up the Manor Social, we'd all pile in with pop, crisps and the latest *Lemon Popsicle* movie on Betamax, with cushions strategically placed to hide any boy embarrassment. We'd laugh our way through the night, always with one eye on the clock until it was time to do one out the back door. The CB radio was massive around this time, nearly every house hold on the estate had one, bit like computers today.

I didn't own one myself, it just wasn't my bag but my sister had a small set in her bedroom, and if my memory serves me well a big f*** off aerial in the back garden. I swear the pole was picking up signals from NASA and the Kremlin. On Fridays after school, and only when the Tube had gone off the box, my mum, sister and I would catch the number 8 bus to the 'Cliffe for our weekly shop at Banners, a basement supermarket in an old Victorian building. It was essential to get the timing right because the number 9 going in the opposite direction back home was on the hour going through Cricket Inn Road, Manor Park and then Manor Lane. If you missed it you had two choices, wait for the next one, or cross the road and get the 52 outside the Spartan Works into town with all the shopping.

It was like being on Dale Winton's supermarket sweep trying to do the shopping in less than an hour and paying for it; in went Weetabix, Cornflakes, tins of soup, bleach, sausages everything crashing into the trolley, not forgetting the orange Club biscuits and Trios I loved so much.

On the few occasions we did miss the bus we'd get the number 52 to the High Street, down the escalator into the Hole In The Road giving the fish in the tank a quick wave before hitting Pond Street for the 56 bus home minus a few Club biscuits and Trios.

Presto supermarket was another favourite of mum's and I also enjoyed the shopping experience too, but not in the way you're thinking... It gave me a great opportunity to gorp at the latest dirty flick that was playing at the Cinecenta. *The Confessions of...* or an *Emmanuelle* erotic film, ahh they don't make 'em like that anymore.

When it came to causing my dear mother grief I had a great track record for never letting her down, but on one occasion I left her frantic with worry whilst still at Wybourn Juniors. One evening I didn't clock in at home till six o'clock, three hours after the final bell had gone, (never did get to ring that bell by the way!)

A mate of mine got wind of a football match taking place at the back of the YEB building across the Parkway, I wasn't sure at first but thought why not, tossing my halo in the nearest bin. The game was a good one, so much so I lost track of the time (well you would with an hour and half each way followed by a next goal winner). Mum went down to school to look for me and enlisted the help of old Tom, the caretaker, who was a diamond geezer. Anyway the both of them searched high and low for me in empty classrooms, cloakrooms, the giant grey bins on wheels and the boiler room the one with the ghost in it. In the end feeling exhausted and helpless mum decided to call those wonderful boys in blue, (tongue in cheek moment there). Just as she opened the door at home to walk across to the phone outside the Windsor, there I was hot footing it down the path covered in fresh grass stains and mud. I got a clip around the afro for my troubles then a huge bear hug and a kiss, I was read the riot act and sent straight to my room, I never realised how much worry I'd caused her and promised not to do it ever again.

Oh and just in case you're wondering we lost 33-32, and had nine goals disallowed.

Meanwhile at the Earls Galf it was thumbs up all round from my teachers as they praised the new improved me, things were looking up and with the mocks coming up I was riding the crest of the highest wave.

But all the praise and thumbs would come crashing down on me as one teacher set out to unsettle my applecart.

The C.F.C

All I ever wanted out of life as a kid was a *Crackerjack* pencil and pen and a cabbage, don't forget the cabbage!

Nearer home it was the end of an era and a massive loss for so many of his friends who loved and worshipped the ground he walked on. Stavros, the local fish and chip proprietor, was going home, a real gentleman and an adopted son of the top end of the estate!

Stav was going to be sorely missed, a prince amongst men. I remember him fondly as always having time for us even when we were being a real pain in the ass, Stav would let us keep warm in the corner of the shop in the winter months sharing a bag of chips between eight or nine of us, which didn't take long to disappear.

Of Greek Cypriot or Cypriot Greek (always important to get the politics right on this one) descent, Stavros turned a deserted rat hole into a clean and modern eaterie with a warm welcome greeting every time you opened the door. Along with his wife and children they made Wybourn their spiritual home, good health Stav, we all miss you.

In his place and heir to the fish supper empire, Rita arrived on the scene with her husband, two daughters, and young son. They lived above the premises just like Stavros did before them and quickly settled into life on a housing estate that never sleeps. It didn't take long for the gossiping to start though, when Rita's husband disappeared into thin air and a new man appeared at the helm frying fish and stinking of batter.

Her 14-year-old daughter set hearts racing and hormones jumping through hoops as she toured the estate making new friends and every lad in the vicinity were trying their luck with the best chat up lines money could buy. But, unbeknown to them, they were wasting their time because she only had eyes for one member of our mob and that was one of my best friends of two on the estate, one who clearly wasn't interested.

She quickly identified me as someone she could talk to and quiz on how best to get inside his head and trousers.

I saw it as a golden opportunity for my pal to lose the big V and told him as much, but a teenage love affair was out of the question. I have to say, he only had himself to blame when the rest of the gang started to question his sexuality, even the empty house with no parents around for days couldn't sway him into taking the plunge. Marie was a really nice girl who became a very good friend, and if it's any consolation sweetheart everyone thought he was mad not to.

My obsession with football continued tenfold as I'd collect anything and everything connected with the round ball game. When the World Cup in Spain was on I collected all of the stickers that were on offer to put inside my Panini sticker book.

Frank, who had the newsagents at the top of Southend Road, needn't have asked what I'd come in for as I burst through the door with my pocket money in my hand. I'd spend the lot on the sweet smelling cards and a copy of that weeks Shoot magazine and, because I was George's son, Frank would let me have a couple more on the house.

My dad and Frank were pretty close pals even though there was an age difference of about ten to fifteen years between them, that didn't matter and the two of them remained tight until my dad left the estate for pastures new.

Over in TV land I was watching loads of it, too much for some peoples' liking. No clues as to who! Laid on the floor with my chin firmly implanted between the palm of my hands and my feet up toasting in front of our gas fire, I watched my favourites of the day. *Top Of The Pops, Runaround* with comic Mike Read, *Rentaghost,* my old mate *Cheggars Plays Pop, Razzamatazz, the Incredible Hulk* and *Grange Hill* with pogo Patterson, Stewpot, and Rolaaaaaand....

Brookside became a must see around this period and only because the love of my life who was introduced a few months earlier made her screen debut...one Tracey Corkhill played by the gorgeous Justine Kerrigan.

After six weeks off I can't think of anyone who would ever look forward to going back to school but I did, I couldn't wait. There was a very good reason for my new found love for Waltheof Comp, and that was the abolition of prison fatigues (the uniform) the ball and chain you just couldn't see. My first day back was fashioned by Adidas Samba trainers, stone washed jeans and a Bad Manners T-Shirt.

Free at last, thank god almighty I'm free at last....

I'd already started my studies just before the holidays, it was designed to give us a taste of what the climate would be like when we returned. I had two years left to shape my future. I'd also got a nice new form teacher in the shape of Mr Wing, of the lab department.

Because of my options I regularly found myself in classes with 'new' pupils, well not exactly new but kids with different form teachers who I'd not been taught with before. Our form stayed as its own unit first thing in the morning and then went our separate ways for the day.

Since we teamed up as rookie 11 and 12-year-olds we'd watched a transition in each other unfold in our unit. Not so long before we arrived at our last educational port of call we were young children. So in effect we'd gone from the "wheels on the bus go round and round" and "hickory dickory dock", to "come on 'av a go if you think you're 'ard enough" and "you're gonna get your f**k** head kicked in".

More often than not I'd stay on for school dinners (with a difference, they were nice). I'd help myself to chips, peas and a huge piece of fish rounded off with two huge slabs of shortbread.

But since hitting the fourth year things had changed, dinnertimes were now spent frequenting the Darnall Libs Social Club which was co-owned by one of my close classmates dad, and after downing a mountain of fish and chips from Darnall Fisheries we'd all pile into the club for games of pool and snooker.

We didn't have to sign in or anything like that, just a quick "I'm with him" did the trick every time leaving the (old) war hero on the door redundant, book and pen at the ready.

It was very rare we arrived back in time for that afternoons lesson because it was a bit of a twat to get a bus back on time. When I was asked where I'd been I'd step to the plate and tell the truth, "I was snookered".

As I mentioned before, the school had a big Asian population of pupils and the few that did integrate with us would receive specialist help from a teacher assigned to help them with the basic skills, like English. It also helped them to tackle society once their schooling was over.

I remember one such teacher who would join our teacher in helping the above mentioned pupils, well that was the plan. Everything seemed to work until the new teacher started getting involved with our schooling, and especially mine. I've got to admit it was all meant well and overall the help wasn't the problem but a battle of wits seemed to ensue.

Things got that bad I ended up with an official complaint against me (grassin'). When I was summoned to the head's office, he was surprised to see me, I'd been out of trouble for so long he thought I'd left, and that was because the new improved me had taken up residency.

I was told that an immediate apology was required, and if I didn't a two week suspension would be passed down.

Two weeks later sentence served, I was back and eager to jump back in the education saddle again.

I never did manage the apology...

Everyone has skeletons in the cupboard and I'm no exception, in fact this one deserves to be, and is on the top shelf with several blankets over it.

I once revealed my secret at a packed two-tone reunion gig, I don't know how loud I was talking but the place went silent and the band stopped playing

I once caught Kajagoogoo live at the Sheffield Lyceum! I couldn't find a confession box anywhere that night so it's been with me ever since, but it sure feels good sharing it with you. I'd actually gone to see a band called Fashion and Limahl and his pals were the support act. The gig was wrapped in controversy because the original lead singer of Fashion had done a runner a few weeks before the tour and most of the assembled crowd knew nothing of it, including me.

So when the curtain went up and a rather rotund bloke in black leather trousers starting belting out the hits, everyone couldn't believe what they were seeing. The bloke's name was Troy something or other, it might have been Tate, not that sure really but if you were there that night have you recovered?

My dad seemed to have had several affairs with clapped out motors over the period; on paper he was a good mechanic but in reality... Dad leave it alone.

Each car bought always needed a fair amount of work on it and tonnes of elbow grease, the car would be near to bits once he'd started and if it wasn't for his good friend and proper mechanic Hank we'd have been tripping over engines, steering wheels and upholstery all day long.

The best motor I ever saw on our estate was local business man and entrepreneur Pete Skinner's roller; the only time you knew he was home from a hard days graft earning pots if it was when he slammed the door shut, otherwise it purred like a kitten.

Staying on the Wybourn, we'd gotten ourselves an unwanted guest. A guest that had been made welcome from the off, but had outstayed it by getting a little too big for his eighteen holers. Along with green pilot jacket, drainpipe jeans, crew cut and an accent that would strip the flaking paint off any bus shelter, he systematically went about signing his own death warrant.

The C.F.C seemed like a nice boy (even Larry would have approved). He was at least five or six years older than us when he started dating one of the local girls on the estate and like I said he was made really welcome in our, and everyone else's circle. Even though we needed an interpreter, he joined in our football games and hung out with us on the Windsor wall. But all the while the C.F.C was plotting to turn the top end of the estate upside down. He'd had several run ins with the local hitters under his belt and there were plenty of stand offs, but nobody twatted him until I got involved in a fracas with him on the tins one afternoon. Everyone started to despise him big time after a few months and it was high time Billy Big Bollocks was taught a lesson, but who was going to do it?

That afternoon me and my good friend had just watched the footy results come in and noticed that the C.F.C's team had lost, not just lost but well and truly wellied into next week. A rampant Fulham side gunning for promotion to the first division under the management of Malcolm (Supermac) Macdonald, the old toon legend, had inflicted the defeat.

Right there and then we decided to save the piss take till later that evening. We went up to the tins for a lark around and then took the path that led you to the castle ruins and the pub where we played football, mainly pairs on a little strip of green but balding grass. In the distance who was sat on the ruins but the C.F.C himself. Well we couldn't resist it flashing the brown and white Vs at him and shouting 4-1, 4-1 at him. As we got closer he leapt up from his stones and slapped my friend round the head sending him flying, I froze on the spot not knowing which way to run as he slapped me in the head, and kicked me right up the arse with his boot.

Now there are some that would say that a Doc Marten boot and a black arse were a perfect match made in heaven (dickheads)!

We both ran off welling up in tears. We reached the bottom of the path that led you back onto Southend Road alongside St Oswalds black railings. As we trooped up the road feeling a little sorry for ourselves the local kingpin was sat on his front step knuckle duster in one hand and Brasso in the other. When he saw us he rose to his feet and asked what was up. As we told him what had happened he reached out for his favourite green stripped Gola trainers and slipped them on and said "lead the way".

When we got to the location the C.F.C was still there wiping the shit off his boots, which was probably mine, when he saw Kingpin coming towards him he didn't flinch, he didn't even try to run away. That's because he knew Kingpin would have tracked him down like an animal to the ends of the earth, so it was best to get it all out of the way.

Kingpin called the two of us over and told the C.F.C that if he ever laid a finger on us again while he was a guest on our turf, he'd turn him inside out and pour salt on him, ouch! After a couple of slaps to the head the C.F.C kind of got the message, then Kingpin turned and walked away into the distance, as we turned to follow we couldn't resist flicking the Vs once more.

This time it was ok, we had protection and although there would be a price to pay somewhere down the line, it was well worth it. I do hope the C.F.C learnt a valuable lesson that afternoon, always find out who your targets are allies with, it could save your life.

Do you want to hear one more story about the C.F.C, he who had a run in with my mum and came off second best? The C.F.C had ruffled one too many feathers which resulted in a showdown with the brother of a girl I attended Waltheof with. The day was set, the time was set, and the venue would be the Windsor courtyard, a real blood and thunder toe to toe. As the two prize fighters traded blows they seemed to be moving all the way down Southend Road, until they suddenly stopped outside the bus shelter and the wholesale butchers opposite my house. They rolled around on the tarmac until they were in the mouth of the keyhole, as they grappled with each other they were locked in battle on the ropes and the ropes were my mum's lovingly tended privet hedge. She went out several times to push them away but was met by an assortment of foul abuse from the C.F.C. so mum went round the back of the house and pulled out a brush with the giant bristles, she gave them one more chance to f*** off and when that didn't work she let the C.F.C have it on the shoulders and back and repeated it every time he fell back into the hedge. It was embarrassing but funny at the same time.

At the end of it all the C.F.C came out on top, but he didn't bank on the younger brother chasing him down Southend Road and probably Wybourn for good.

I couldn't wait for Saturday afternoons because that meant the Alpine pop lorry would be in town, so to speak. It toured the estate top and bottom selling bottles of pop, you could get about five for a quid or so, orange, strawberry, cola, lemonade and my favourite Dandy and Burdock.

The blokes on the back of the wagon wouldn't have looked out of place on Simon Cowell's *Britain's Got Talent* the way they threw the bottles to each other, full and empties without breaking any glass.

The one thing I remember about Tom's van was that it wasn't very big, but whatever you wanted it was in the back. Then there was Harry and his Fletchers van that drove into the keyhole every morning, I'd stock up on big bags of buns then dispose of the lot in one single sitting.

Remember when I told you there'd be a price to pay for Kingpin's added protection from the C.F.C? Well that day came one afternoon when he knocked at the door. I was home alone which was just as well because my mum would have smelt a giant rat. Turns out Kingpin was calling in the favour, and I was ok with that just as long as it didn't involve a sawn off and a used pair of Pretty Polly tights.

He wanted me to keep something for him or hide it for a few days and handed me a huge bundle of bubble wrap and brown tape; there was no way of guessing what was inside, he'd wrapped it up well. Let's just say in any pass the parcel game it would have taken at least two hundred children to get through it. He explained that he'd tip me the wink when he was ready to take back his possession, so I set about laying it to rest in the garden next to mum's roses.

When the day came to give up the bubble wrap and brown tape I told him where it was, but he wanted me to leave my orange football at X marks the spot. He would then creep into the garden in the dead of night like a thief on the Wybourn and dig it up. I couldn't sleep that night and kept looking out of the window, but my ball was still there. I must have dropped off in the night because when I woke up and looked through the window mum was in the garden, hands on hips.

My first thought was "oh shit and quickly dived into my Scooby Doo jim jams. As I approached the spot mum was staring down a rather big hole, she couldn't understand it and I pretended I couldn't understand it either. In the end I tried to blame it on the local cats, you know what they're like. But I was stumped by the f***** shovel standing upright in the dirt, I mean come on how many cats do you know that dig their own shitholes with a shovel? Nice one Kingpin, and where's my ball?

One afternoon I was coming out of the shop now owned by Mr and Mrs Khan when three Brookies (Waltheof's deadly rivals from Brook School on the Manor) approached me.

Before I knew it I was sucker punched flush on the chin by a crushing right to the jaw that would have floored Leonard, Hagler, Hearns and Roberto Duran all at once.

There was blood and Monster Munch everywhere.

Mrs Khan came out of the shop and swept up all the crisps before quickly heading back towards the door.

Thanks Mrs K, I'll be fine.

To be fair she did come out again, even if it was only to hand me back my teeth.

Anyway the reason I tell you this is because when I told the lads they couldn't wait to avenge my misfortune. We marched up to Southend Road and headed in the direction of the Manor.

I was at the back nursing a fatter lip when all of a sudden I was overcome with emotion. My friends who were leading the charge on my behalf were the same lads who had watched open mouthed as me and my family moved into number 52 Southend Road.

We'd started out as aliens from a different planet and now here we were as one, ten years later. When I first moved onto the estate the kids I used to hang with were becoming distant memories, we'd just drifted off with different mates. Thankfully we'd see each other in passing and there was still that mutual respect for each other.

Now in the beginning I tried not to name names, simply because there's always somebody or someone you might forget to mention, but I'm going to be brave and do it anyway.

And if I do leave anybody out, there are plenty of pages left to rectify things. So the first mob rogues gallery reads like this...

My neighbour and good friend Paul Curry, Andrew Smart, Lee Legdon, Anthony Bernard, Mark Wrigley, Matt Simpson, Scott and Jamie Middleton, Paul Skinner, Darren Parkin, Ian Walkland, lee Hitchen, John Loukes, Gavin Furniss, Mark Andrews, Robert Beckingham, Bod Adams, Paul Allsopp and lucky dog.

In 1983, Sally Ride went up in space, 'Karma Chameleon' was on everybody's lips and I had one more term to serve at Waltheof Comp, but how would it all end? Your guess is as good as mine.

See you after the holidays...

Kappa (Jumpers For Goalposts)

The older boys (sorry), slightly older boys, on the Windsor wall were now ready to make way for its new generation of youthful hell raisers; after all they'd already been there, done that, and made off with the T-shirts. The likes of Mark Reilly, Eli, Barry Creaser, Mo and Abbey, Nobby, Rammy, Gary and Brian Rasdale, Dinky and Tony Dawson, Big Shane, Andy Broughton, Masher Hurst, Mina and Nicholas Highfield.

As young lads we'd listened in wide eyed and excited as they relayed the tales of the drunken night before, Steelys, knee tremblers and kebabs.

It all sounded great but at this early stage in our careers we were still on the kid pops and crisps, we'd have to wait that little bit longer for a round of John Smiths and a packet of dry roasted.

The big V was still intact and I was desperate to lose it, and I really thought it would happen with a little number I'd met off Maltravers Road who used to hang with us. Her old man was from Saudi, her mum was English and I tell you what, I was all over it, I was always making her laugh either she thought I was funny, or just stupid, I don't know, but for one shining moment I thought first base was within touching distance.

After a while we'd start sloping off from the rest of the gang (ripping them off that was the term back then made even worse if you were ripping off for female company). The lads always came first, but on this occasion they didn't stand a chance.

I'd make some excuse about having to go in and I'd walk off into the distance and through the front gate straight out the back again and over the back field to meet her in the centre circle on St Oswalds football pitch. Once there we'd laugh, joke and generally fool around, on more than one occasion when I was getting a little too carried away with myself she'd tell me she was saving herself for someone special.

Talk about a slap in the chops, that girl really knew how to make a boy feel good about himself. If at any time you were walking the dog or ferret and you heard screams, squeals, and cries for help coming from the middle of the field, that was me, she kept it together at all times.

Clothing was an important part of our progression into young men about town in the early to mid-eighties as a string of shops appeared in the city centre that catered for the fashion gurus amongst us.

Some of the shops, it has to be said, had existed for years, but even they could see the huge potential in stocking what the young men and women were starting to crave.

JD Sports, Olympus Sport, Next, Benetton and even Suggs Sport with Horn Bros bringing up the rear, were queuing up to take hold of the newest and latest fashion trends.

Fila, Lacoste, Kappa, Ellesse, Henri Lloyd, Lyle and Scott, Tachini, Patrick and old favourite, Nike, were labels that were popping up everywhere and very soon the young youth of the day would be buying into it by the truckload. At the time no one knew where it had all started, there were always conflicting reports of Liverpool and Manchester, but wherever the origin, those threads were heaven sent.

Liverpool fans have since laid claim to starting the whole scene off by bringing back the top gear bought or stolen from their many exploits in Europe in the late '70s early '80s.

My favourite outfit was blue and white Gazelle trainers, brown Wrangler cords with frayed bottoms, blue Kappa jumper, plain red polo and deer stalker. The colour of my skin wasn't enough to make me stand out, but that get up did the trick and then some. So like I said before, the old guard were on their way out and the new bloods were coming in, which yielded such names as, your truly, Terry and Lee Coleman, Lee Herriot, Tom Ward, Steve Jones, Sean Hancock, Wayne (Trendy) Sharp, Nigel and Neil Highfield, Drin and Nicky White, Paul Vice, Karl Glossop, Chris Lambing, Gav Furniss, Paul Skinner, Wayne (Archie) Marsden, Dave Cross, John Turner and Maurice Melia. And it was these band of brothers that would form the nucleus of our early steps onto the Sheffield nightlife scene of the 1980s.

On more than one occasion I've pointed out that I'm a real football nut, and it's around this time I started watching Sheffield Wednesday Football Club with my best friend of two on the estate. I've always had a soft spot for the blue half of Sheffield and during the 1983/84 season me and my pal went everywhere watching the Owls. Lyons, Varadi, Bannister, Megson, Sterland, Hodge, Shelton etc. etc. were on the successful road to promotion into Division One, under the management of Howard Wilkinson. On most of the away days you'd meet some real colourful characters; the good, the bad, and the downright 'orrible.

One lad who I thought was a real cool kid was Mad Booker who never seemed to miss a game, home or away. Some people thought he was a real wild one, but he was alright by me. At the height of the football hooliganism epidemic in Britain, there were some scary and hairy moments mixed in with the euphoria of another two points (yes two points! For you younger readers) on the road.

In Newcastle our police escort didn't show as hundreds of Yorkshire men were left to fend for themselves on the platforms and believe me when I tell you it was no accident. Sometimes the police would take great pleasure in watching that week's visitors get a good kicking, and would only step in when the away support had no fight left in them.

That was football in the 1980s, even the coppers were villains. On another occasion a group of us went over to Manchester City's Maine Road and decided to make our own way there. We didn't realise when we got there that we'd just done the unofficial tour of the Moss Side estate, we were totally oblivious. There were some very funny moments though, police on horseback had never sat well with me, the way they plough through the crowd as if they're not there. This time the crowd were outside the turnstiles ready to part with their well-earned, when a horse suddenly lifted its tail and sprayed its bowels all over the poor buggers waiting patiently in line. Whether the horse ate a dodgy curry the night before, we don't know but I bet those poor lads never got a lift back on the coach home to Sheffield. On a more serious note, the ugly side of racism in football in the '80s reared its ugly head when in one game big Bob Hazel was getting some right stick off the Wednesdayites. The usual monkey chants and the old "ooh ooh ooh" were directed toward Bob when one supporter turned to me and said, and I quote "not you pal your one of ours". At 14-years-old I was far too young to nail him on the bridge of his nose, sending him rolling down the away end. While I'm on the subject I'd like to pay tribute to some of the pioneering black footballers who took it all in their stride with a smile, and their self-discipline intact. Take a bow Cunningham, Regis, Best, Hilaire, Crookes, Moses, Berry, Anderson, Connor, Gayle, Canoville, Blisset, Barnes and the hundreds I haven't name checked, your my heroes.

For an FA Cup quarter final tie with Southampton at Hillsborough, my sister made us a massive banner, it had four small owls in each corner and a huge owl in the middle.

The best bit about that banner was that it was all hand embroidered, every last stitch. The game was live on the BBC so the plan was to drape it over the fencing on the kop, and every time the ball went out of play and Peter Shilton prepared to take his kick there it was in all its glory.

Back at Waltheof HQ, it was seconds out round one. In the blue corner yours truly and in the red corner, another teacher-style adversary. We disagreed on everything. I found the teacher's whole approach to teaching amateurish and pompous, the only thing we did agree on was when it was time to leave at the end of the lesson.

Chemistry (and there was little of that between us) just wasn't my bag. Having ditched the school uniform the pupils were turning up for school in some really awful and downright bizarre outfits, the new romantic crowd with their frilly gloves and eyeliner were real head turners. The metal kids just carried on with the denims covered in patches sporting their favourite bands of the time, Rainbow, Whitesnake, Saxon and Motorhead. Us rude boys were now sporting the trendy look Kappa, Ellesse etc etc and smart colourful trainers, Gazelles mainly but my best friend took things to the extreme by going all neo Nazi on me, but please let me explain.

Dr Marten eighteen holers, banana yellow sta-prest trousers, black pilot jacket and a gruesome shave of the bonce, he was always going to get himself noticed. And noticed he was, he looked as though he was on his way to a National Front fundraiser, only he was innocently on his way to school with his books tucked neatly under his arm.

And not a single copy of Mein Kampf in sight!

One morning he called round as usual and waited for me whilst I tended to my afro in the mirror when I caught sight of his coloured laces that he'd purchased from the Friday morning market.

He was now showing his allegiance to the National Front, I knew it, my sister knew it, but just for the hell of it and for a few laughs we didn't let on, he was clueless. And with a huge Asian population of pupils in attendance, I was about to have me a really fun day.

My education was back on the slippery slope. I'd fallen off the wagon and straight back into the path of my old ways of not wanting to do what I was told and becoming lazy and disruptive once again. To counter the problem I was taken out of the lessons and made to work on my own with, and there is no other word for it, a teaching babysitter who I grew to loathe with a passion. Mr Nicholson was from over the border, a brave heart, and he and I went at it from the off. He thought he knew what was best for me but he hardly knew me at all, the school's resident expert in nothing. Sometimes I would forget about the solitary bit and attend class as usual, only for brave heart to come crashing through the door and demanding my presence. Even when I was hard at it eyes down he'd still insist on me joining him.

The school thought I needed to see a shrink, and that's exactly what happened, which makes me sound like a right fruit and nut case but I was referred to a specialist in unruly juvenile behaviour on Ecclesall Road, there, that sounds a whole lot better don't it? Will the round shape fit into the square, what do you see when you look at the picture etc etc? Those were the crazy things and questions I was being asked in each and every session as I played them for the fools they were.

I bet they were on a right earner trying to scramble my brain into tiny pieces before putting the fragments back together again. Money for nothing and nice work if you can get it. I can't remember how many couch sessions there were, but I'm sure at the end of it all the conclusion was I was just your average everyday rabble rouser.

In one particular lesson a teacher who had shown me great kindness previously, went down in my estimation, right down to the bottom of the barrel. As usual we were in fine voice and displaying all the attributes of a pack of PG Chimps at a tea party, the teacher in question couldn't quite get himself heard or noticed for that matter, as we carried on as if he wasn't there. I had mixed feelings about the commotion because I liked the fella, then all of a sudden he slammed his books down on the table and rounded on a mate and fellow Wybourner.

This one involves my mate and fellow Wybourner again, only this time it was the new girl giving him a good bashing, this time of the earholes. She waltzed into the year like a local gunslinger on a mission hell bent on cleaning up dodge. Now if someone were to tell me she used to be a man, I'd seriously take them at their word because she could have worked any number of nightclub door and coupled with a snarl that would've had those lovable Kray twins crying for mummy, nobody was going to stop her reaching top girl status. But in her quest for the top job, there was something missing, and that was a top boy right by her side.

At first glance she set her eagle like eyes on my mate, who quickly fell under her spell and thumb, and for a crazy while she thought she'd hit the jackpot. He was into joining the army, talked a good fight, and had no fear (except for Mr Lovett of course) but all that changed when she found out he didn't even register in the top one hundred of nasty bastards. It didn't help his cause much when Bev and Jane made the top twenty big hitters in the school. So then she turned her attention to our other classmate and cock of the year, but she was left humiliated and disappointed when he gave her short shrift and laughed in her face.

Yet undeterred she then came a knocking at the door of deputy and second in line to the top boy crown, who I have to say was also a decent lad, quiet and reserved. But even he like my mate before him and I would imagine countless others before them, fell for her vice like charms.

From then on everyone and everything was going along great until one morning she must have woke up and thought number one girl and number two boy didn't seem right. Boyfriend would have to up his game, and claim the coveted number one slot, but how?

There was trouble brewing that's for sure as she did her best Don King impression trying to promote the rumble in the Manor, a winner takes all slugfest. Thankfully that's where it all ended as number one and number two put their heads together and quashed any talk of fighting, and for what? So Cruella could get her kicks, thanks but no thanks.

I do hope she didn't have any children, especially boys because she'd probably have them entering the ring fighting for the biggest bedroom.

The death of someone so young must be one of the bitterest pills to take, I can't begin to imagine how that must feel for any family involved in such sorrowful circumstances.

Jamie Sharman was one of the original metal kids who had enrolled in the second year at the same time as me, and although I didn't get to know him properly until two years in, his untimely passing did have a shattering affect on me.

We had joined forces in geography with Mr Grundy as part of our options, and I found him a quiet but often funny kinda guy. In the early years the rude boys and the metal kids used to slag each others music tastes off like young men do, and he would always be there flying the metal flag.

When the news was broken in a packed assembly hall, it didn't quite sink in, the school and some of its pupils including Jamie had gone off on a skiing trip.

Most of them who I knew as well were in high spirits, and really looking forward to the experience, without going into too much detail young Jamie never came home having met with an accident that claimed his young life. Like I said I didn't know him till we became classmates in geography, but the news hit hard all the same simply because he was so young, you're supposed to live your life till a ripe old age and experience life, not have it cut short before its even began.

I'll never forget him nor will Waltheof Comprehensive School. I hope the tree that was planted in the school grounds in his honour rises to the heavens, where he lay in eternal peace forever.

With only a few months to go and those all important A and O level exams on the horizon time was running out, and the pressure on, what was I to do? I knew I'd blown any chances I had of ever achieving my goal, and if the truth be known I just wanted out. Looking back at that important time in my life I'd as good as pissed my education up the school walls, any chances I ever had of making something of myself were well and truly over, or were they? There was something out there that would turn me around, kick me up the backside and change the way I felt about the whole education system. Something that would change my views and overall outlook on life…

All Aboard The Thatcher Express.... Fare 26.25

The Soviet Union were going through its leaders like they were going out of fashion, the Ruskies had seen three of its key figures, Brezhnev Andropov and Chernenko, all die in office, and all with one thing in common and that was trying to stay one step ahead of Reagan's America in the post war nuclear arms race.

Yes folks these were scary times we were living in, that little red button cast a huge shadow over the world as hostilities intensified between the two great superpowers. But it couldn't happen here, could it? One thing was for sure as I sat up and took notice of the real possibility of World War Three, I would never ever again pour scorn on the women of Greenham Common.

One afternoon in Mr Evans' economics class, we entered the room to find a TV set in position for the screening of a little known film/drama called *Threads* ('great I'll get the popcorn').

It told the story of the aftermath of a nuclear explosion and the affect it would have on the citizens of Sheffield in the event of the dreaded mushroom cloud ever looming large over South Yorkshire. All of a sudden the popcorn joke wasn't funny anymore, as we sat down cross legged awaiting our future fate, I can't remember all the film nor do I want to but the odd occasional flashback sticks in my mind, like the old lady that wet herself when the cloud appeared and the commotion in the streets.

One other notable scene from the film was when the whole of Kelvin flats came tumbling down into a pile of grey rubble (and your problem with that was?); all in all it was for most of us, even the hard nuts, the most frightening piece of film we'd ever seen, the place fell silent till the very end even after the credits rolled there was a hush you'd never heard before or since.

When Mr Evans pulled back the curtains he told us to go enjoy your dinners, what! The man was off his head if he thought anyone could keep anything down after that carnage.

The Americans are coming, well at least they were in our house as the shows from across the pond dominated our television set, night and day, day and night. If it wasn't mum with her weekly dose of *Dallas, Dynasty* and *Knots Landing* with a little *Sons and Daughters* mixed in (and yes I do know the latter was Australian) there was no let up.

I also weighed in with some time honoured classics such as, *Magnum Pi, TJ*

Hooker, Different Strokes, Big John, Little John, Fame, Welcome back Kotter, Starsky and Hutch and *Petrocelli.* I loved *Petrocelli,* he was a lawyer trying to build his own house, and in each episode he'd lay a brick then get called away on an important case. And that's the way the show opened every week, he'd lay the brick and then get called away, classic.

And yet with all those class shows on offer, the best was yet to come and in its wake would change the way British men would dress for the next five years.

On the music front I was becoming pretty diverse at listening to any good music that was on offer, before it was two-tone or nothing at all, but the barriers had been taken down and now admission was free. So welcome to my world, ABC's 'Lexicon of Love', Human League's 'Dare' album and Scritti Politti 'Asylums in Jerusalem' which I had borrowed from a sixth former at school.

I failed to get my grades needed to test myself in the murky world of journalism, albeit sport; I knew it was coming so it didn't come as any surprise to me when I opened the official looking envelope that read scrapheap on the front.

It was time to take stock and decide what was next, but before all that there was a school leaving disco to attend, and one last look at the place that had held me captive with no parole in the offing for four years. I sure as hell wasn't going to miss that.

Some of my teachers were ok I suppose, like Mr Norris. I once toyed with the idea of getting a scooter so I joined his road safety motorbike classes. You should have seen me tearing around the school on a orange Honda Hairdryer bike with a stupid basket on the front of it and a white helmet as big as the moon on my head.

Mr Macaddam was my favourite teacher, he and I got on really well, he understood me and I him, how you doin Sir?

Mrs Shaw, when I first started she was known to me as the dear old bat, four years on and she was like my favourite grandmother, Hi miss.

Miss Potts, what can I say that hasn't already been said, you were wonderful.

So on the eve of the disco my mate took possession of a mohair jumper my sister had knitted for him to wear on the big night, it suited him down to the ground, in fact it was so thick Scott of the Antarctic would have put it straight into his case on his ill fated trip to the North Pole.

Never in my wildest dreams did I ever imagine shedding a tear for the old maze prison (Waltheof) I'd grown rather fond of the place, even though it was on its last legs, and falling down around our ears. But most of all I was going to miss my friends, no longer my mates, but my friends. I've tried my best to remember you all, but there are one or two of you I can see in my head but can't quite put a name to, if it's you "hello and good times my friend".

Not everyone will have surnames in print, simply because I don't remember, no disrespect intended, so here goes!

Simon Taylor, Dino Thompson, Paul (pele) Thompson, Alan Perry, David Bates, Dennis Blinco, Timothy Atkinson, Peter Houghton, Mark Fletcher, Russ (Larry) Grayson, Yen, Chris Beaumont, Mick Burkinshaw, Wayne Damms, Paul Coleshill, Darren Foster, Maxine Watts, Tracey Sampson, Lynne Smith, Claire Faram, Beverly Bullivant, Tracey (cruella) Stacey, Shaneal Huckstepp (is that right Shazza?) Tina, Debbie, Julie, Fiona, Shazia and Paul McCann.

Wow, including me, by today's standards that would be seen as over-crowding of the classroom, and there are still three absentees to account for (waggin' it) again.

So back to the disco, and what an emotional night it was, the laughing, the hugging, the kissing and not forgetting the dancing took place in the assembly hall. My best and favourite memory of the night was seeing my friend struggle with the mohair jumper under the heat of the lights coupled with the mass of heaving bodies.

He had nothing on underneath so the sweat and the strands of mohair combined made it a really uncomfortable night for him, and where was I as he struggled with fashion? On my knees mate, doubled up with tears of laughter running down my face.

So many goodbyes made it a really teary night and I'm not ashamed to admit that, I was going to miss them all.

At the end of the night as we approached the white wooden fence that had penned us in for so long, I turned to face the school one more time and saluted her and that's no lie, I saluted the best years of my life so far..

In the summer of '84, I decided I was going to relax (cue Frankie) and unwind, I was in no hurry to chain myself to a machine or any other mechanical apparatus for a long while yet.

Most of my mates on the estate had gone off to work at Richardson's, Sheffield's cutlery experts, but that didn't appeal to me even though it meant cash in my pocket.

So that summer I lazed around in the day and played football by night; at the weekends we'd make the short trip over to the back of the Manor Park Centre to take on Paul and Micky Connors team. We beat them all of the time, although I think the pair of them might tell you a different story, how you doing boys? As the summer was nearing its sunshine end, I applied to Granville College to study in depth all the exams I'd sensationally bombed out at Waltheof, but there was disappointment when I was told all courses were full, I'd left things a little too late.

I got the same answer from Shirecliffe too, so I went to my careers officer who was a knockout brunette to see what she could do for me. After a lot of phone calls and running around she found me a place at Stocksbridge College, just one question though, where the hell was that?

The number 57 bus stopped outside the dreaded Sheaf Valley Baths in Pond Street, and as I boarded the bus I wondered what I was letting myself in for.

The journey took me through Hillsborough, Middlewood, Wharncliffe and Deepcar, after that it was dry stoned walls, green fields and livestock. By now I was starting to panic a little, had I missed my stop, surely man couldn't exist out here!

I can clearly remember asking the bus driver are we there yet? When I did finally alight from the bus it seemed as though I was in a different world, I was only a few miles from Manchester for Christ sake, which really spooked me no end.

The kids, or should I say students now, were mainly from the Wharncliffe Side estate and of course Stocksbridge area, very posh looking and sounding souls, but friendly all the same.

I hung out with two black kids from the Pitsmoor end of town and couldn't understand a word they were saying half the time. On a good day I'd laugh when they laughed, kissed my teeth when they did, and high fived when I thought it appropriate (fuck me I'd well and truly lost my identity, "thanks mum") Two girls from the new Waterthorpe estate near Beighton joined us as we all caught the bus and hung out throughout the day. The girls made me laugh because they dressed exactly the same and had the same haircuts, and listened to the same music. They were twins, well almost one was black the other white.

The journey up there was beginning to take its toll on me, it was an early start and an even later finish, I was shagged out by the time I got home. I would fall asleep in my plate of rice and peas, something had to give, my young health was at risk. I applied once again for Granville College and this time a few openings had become available, so I grabbed the chance with both hands. Granville was a half a house brick throw away from home so for me it was a right result, the John O' Groats to Lands End epic trek was over.

The Government grants back then were really hard to come by, and I was running out of flash money, so my friends suggested I join a Government backed YTS programme while still attending college. I thought it was a great idea, but there was one stumbling block, I had no record, no wrap sheet, I had never been in any bovver with the law. Nacro was where most of my pals were at a YTS scheme for the bad lads of Sheffield, and I was seen as to squeaky clean. (never a handbag around when you need one!)

It had been a pretty eventful 1984, not just at home, but overseas as well, the world was changing, some said for the better, but the doom merchants were always on hand to differ.

Mrs Ghandi was assassinated, Richard Burton said his last farewell to Liz, Skating duo Torvill and Dean wowed us in Sarajevo, Gary Hart was bidding to topple Ronald Reagan as the next commander in Chief. Count Basie died, York Minister went up in flames, Carl Lewis ran the show at the Olympics and the IRA fluffed their lines in Brighton. The Miners' Strike was headline news in '84 as King Arthur and his followers took on the might of the Thatcher government and her plans for the mass genocide of the British industry as we knew it.

At the turn of the year I joined Sheffield Starting Point, a YTS programme on the Wicker behind Bennet's fishing tackle shop.

Half the Wybourn lads were on it and I felt right at home the moment Avril the blonde bombshell buzzed me in at reception. There were a multitude of trades to try out from joinery, bricklaying, and plastering to pastel design and economics (cookin'). I settled on painting and decorating with Ray Shaw which I really enjoyed, and have kept those skills with me to this day.

Boxing trainer and legend Brendan Ingle was a popular figure around the place as he was a team leader, along with his then protégé Brian Anderson. Bomber Graham would pop his head round the door every once in a while which got the whole place buzzing as Bomber was one of the most recognisable faces around Sheffield at the time. I do admit to falling for the pranks designed at keeping the new starter on his toes though, and I'd challenge anyone who says they didn't. The long stand, the tartan paint and the glass hammer were just some of the equipment I was sent to fetch from the stores room.

On paydays we'd all gather on mass on the Wicker, then make our way up to the High Street and head straight for the Leeds Building Society to collect our £26.25. It was hardly worth the effort of putting it in there, as cash would have done us nicely.

Every Thursday morning I bet the staff at the Leeds braced themselves for donkey jackets, muddy boots and some very choice language indeed. So along with learning a trade and sitting my O levels again, things were looking up, but (and there's always a but) the strong arm of the law threatened to blot my copybook.

There was quite a number of girls off Wybourn at Starting Point and one of them I'd known since nursery, then juniors and we both attended Waltheof together, so she was no stranger.

Her friend was a real ball breaker, but underneath it all a heart of gold, but

90

you still wouldn't mess with her regardless. Ball breaker had invited us all to her brother's birthday bash (18th or 21st, I can't remember which) at a local watering hole on Attercliffe. On the night in question, we piled into the Windsor for a few before moving on in a fleet of taxis to the 'Cliffe. When we arrived you could smell the hostility in the air, I don't know why but I could smell trouble and sausage rolls, when we went upstairs to attack the bar and buffet, the Tinsley lads were already there.

Stuffing their fat faces like there was no tomorrow, we knew one or two of them from the Point, but after that there was no love lost. The night went well, or so it seemed, everyone was having a really good time until something (and I don't know what) triggered it all off. We fancied our chances in a food fight but a toe to toe would have been suicide because they had a huge black lad with them who must have been Mike Tyson's mould, he was f**kin' huge. So as the atmosphere turned sour I'm not ashamed to say Wybourn did a runner straight out of the pub onto the empty streets of Attercliffe.

I was fuming as I'd just filled a huge paper plate of grub and now I was leaving it behind for someone else to devour it.

In everyone's frustration some of the boys started to get a bit loud and larey, suddenly my mate picked up a huge house brick and launched it straight through the window of Hitchen's department store, leaving the mannequins cowering in the corner of the display.

After that everyone shot off up Staniforth Road but me and two other mates decided not to run but walk straight toward Hyde Park Flats. We'd only taken a few steps when the flashing blue light of a Z Car came screeching to a halt at the side of us. We were then asked where we were going and where we had been, then the other officer asked the million dollar question, "who smashed up the shop front?" "

We told him we didn't know, but they weren't buying any of it. Then one officer disappeared and came back with his star witness. You couldn't make up what happened next, the witness pointed to me and told the officer, "that's him".

I couldn't believe it, I turned to my right and then to my left, then behind me, I was looking for the *Game For A Laugh* team with Jeremy Beadle at the forefront of the joke. But it was no joke, I was done up like a kipper, my mates pleaded with the coppers to let me go as I wasn't the guilty party, but it was no use, I was on my way to the jailhouse. You have to remember this was the 1980s and the black youth of the day was seen as public enemy number one, the riots a few years before had seen to that.

In my humble opinion I reckon the police at that time must have been on some kind of bonus for every black face they pulled in, and by pulling me in they'd probably just earned themselves a weekend trip to Paris for two. Together I suspect. And all at my expense!..

I was proper brickin' it now, I'd heard about the old mattress and truncheon routine and feared for my good looks and safety, in that order. When I was put into the car it was routine for the copper to place his hand on top of your head so you didn't have a nasty bump on the way in.

So when he put his hand on my head to do just that I nearly pissed myself laughing when he withdrew his hand that was now covered in Brylcreem and half a ton of gel.

When I got to the station , the station officer could see I was a little shaken so he decided not to slam the cell door shut, I still had to take my laces out of my Gazelles though which really pissed me off, because they were going to be a real twat to put back in.

I must have sobbed myself to sleep, which is surprising given the blanket they gave me; hadn't these people ever heard of Lenor fabric conditioner? It was like sleeping with a Brillo pad.

When I was questioned I could sense they knew it wasn't me, so they kept asking me to give him up, my mate, but there was no chance of that. Number one, never grass and number two, my mate would have gone straight into a Borstal type residence for sure because he'd already used up eight of nine lives. When they gave up on stitching me up I was told I could walk, the arresting pair looked gutted, "put those passports away fellas". But not to be outdone the gruesome twosome decided they would take me home, even though I told them I'd make my own way.

They weren't stupid those two, they knew the stigma attached to any black family with involvement with the police; people would talk. As we approached home the flashing blue light was put on just for show, luckily for me and my parents it was the early hours of the morning so most of my neighbours would have been counting sheep rustlers.

The morning after I got up and gave a huge sigh of relief, I was untouched and unmarked. On the Windsor that afternoon I was given a few slaps on the back for not committing the cardinal sin of turning supergrass. I'd taken one for the team and it wasn't going to be forgotten.

Out of the six exams I sat, I did very well in four and got an average grade in the fifth, number six, let's not even go there.

That summer on a bright sunny evening, hundreds of Wybourners and the residents of Sky Edge sat on top of the hill for a musical concert that could be heard loud and clear from Sheffield United's Bramall Lane. The boss was in town.

Bruce Springsteen and his E Street band rocked Sheffield to its foundations when the American rockers' European tour hit South Yorkshire.

'Glory Days', 'Cover Me' and American standard 'Born In The USA' filled the night sky as we freeloaders partied till the early hours, downing cans of lager and bottles of Woodpecker.

And that wasn't the only time that summer the lane had seen such numbers flocking through its turnstiles. American Evangelist Billy Graham did a week long stint there and thousands upon thousands from across the globe came to see and listen to him, the Parkway was choca with coaches as far as the naked eye could see.

It was time to start hitting the town, we'd waited long enough to sample the delights of the Sheffield nightlife scene, and could wait no more. It was baby steps at first, and after a few wobbles and falls we hit the ground running. I'd started shaving now but still hadn't mastered the art of not slashing my cheeks to bits, on some days it looked like I had tiny Japanese flags all over my face! See you at the bar, cheers.

Bloomers, And The Lady In White

Never in a million years did I ever think the Miners' Strike would affect my life. Never in a million years did I think the Miners' Strike would affect my love life, but it did on both counts.

There seemed to be a really annoying mod revival around this time. Every estate in Sheffield was saturated with the sixties throwbacks, and our estate didn't escape the deluge either.

Most of the mods were off the top end of Manor and would congregate outside the Ritz video shop on City Road, which became a no go area for a while.

Back in the day it was the rockers who duelled with the fish tail parker gang, but in '85 the trendy became their arch enemies. The trouble started when one or two ordinary boys, Gazelle trainers and the like, took a few clips round the lugholes outside the City Road cemetery. And it didn't stop there, if anyone returning the latest Stallone video blockbuster back to Ritz who thought they were going to get an easy ride from the brain deads, were very sadly mistaken. Enough was enough, and things came to a head when at least three hundred or more trendys gathered on Fargate to confront the mods who had taken up residency on the bandstand on the Moor. There was a lot of toing and froing as to who should lead the line, and in the end a lad called China got the job.

The trendys then set off from Fargate, through the Town hall courtyard, past the eggbox and down onto the brow of the Moor - only to be confronted by a row of police officers.

The fuzz seemed to relish the prospect of more Orgreave-style head bashing, they were in no mood to let anyone through, but I bet they were itching for someone to try.

There then followed a stand off that lasted for over an hour, with neither side willing to budge, the mods got off scot free that day, the trendsetters were really chompin' at the bit.

Ahh! Live Aid, and anyone who was anyone was going to be there, bar us. Well, we'll soon see about that.

We hatched an audacious plan to get down there via the Parkway, the M1 and our thumbs out. In my mate's garden shed we got hold of two big pieces of cardboard and with a pot of black paint and a brush daubed London in huge letters all over it, simple.

But we argued on which way the arrow should go, I reasoned that if we went on

94

the side leading south the arrow should go the same way, but it's hard to judge when you're doing it on the floor of a garden shed.

Anyway, on the morning of the biggest gig in the world we crossed over to the other side of the Parkway, but guess what, the arrow was pointing the wrong way, we were now Glasgow bound, so we turned it upside down which meant we were now on our way to NODNO7. After an hour that seemed like ten, we knocked it on the head and went our separate ways home, it was a daft idea anyhow no tickets no money and no idea.

I watched most but not all of it on the box and have since watched it in its entirety, and who could argue with Queen being the stars of the show, Awesome…

Baby steps aside, we the lads, the faces, started to take in more pubs close to town but were still reluctant to cross the bridge at Sheaf Market to sample the Cannon, Garden and Marples. Instead we all piled into the Ball which was our good mates mum and dad's boozer opposite Granelli's, and were made welcome every time we wandered in. The Durham Ox and Ye Olde Arrow were also on the map.

I loved it in the Ball, we'd hog the dartboard, snooker and pool tables and the bandit from opening to chuckin' out. On some occasions you'd get the odd bird in off the Park Hill flats, but more often than not we knew them.

The day we made our way into town, is a night I'll never forget. Archie, Nigel Highfield, Lee (Ronnie) Coleman, Terry Coleman, Lee Herriott, Gav Furniss, Wayne Sharp, Nicky White and yours truly made the cross over from young upstarts to fashionable young gentlemen about town. For me personally I was like a kid in that sweetie shop, there was high heels, legs and pretty girls everywhere, I thought I'd died, been nailed in and already at heaven's gate.

The Cannon downstairs, if you can remember, had a huge spacious bar that looked as though it was modelled like the inside of the City Hall's Oval Hall, and that became our starting point. We'd stay in for a few, then go up to the Old Blue Bell which rocked on a Saturday night, after that we'd go into what would become my favourite haunt, Legends.

The Wig and Pen, which reminded me of stepping onto a canal barge was a firm favourite too, I once knocked myself out on the low wooden beams that seemed to hold the Sheffield establishment up. The Golden Ball was a cracking place, always rammed with revellers and more importantly girls. It was a real nightmare getting served at the bar and I'd often get pushed to the front by the lads to get the beers in, I was towering at this point and still growing, the sky's the limit.

Next stop was the Stonehouse, the scene for many a twisted ankle with its cobbles and potholes that came with the Victorian Street theme that they had going on. In fact if you were a little worse for drink you would have never have made it up the steep little road leading up to the High Street, the Job Centre and of course the Stonehouse, that led you up from the Golden's doors.

I also loved the Mulberry Tavern, it was small and congested downstairs and small and congested upstairs, often a tight squeeze but we never complained about that with seventy-five percent of the crowd drop dead women.

Marples was nearly everyone's favourite pre club bar nothing to look at from outside but inside a den for the great unwashed, a terrific atmosphere and a fantastic DJ.

In the early days our next stop would have been Bloomers, another pre club outlet that was attached to Turn Ups nightspot on Commercial Street.

I always felt that Bloomers could have held its own in the other half of the town centre, it was a pristine and well-kept bar, it could have easily stood side by side with Henry's no probs.

Now I'm going to tell you how difficult it was for the young black yoot in the mid '80s, to walk straight into any Sheffield nightspot without any hassle from the over zealous Bouncers (hang on they don't even deserve a capital letter), bouncers.

How difficult? About as difficult as keeping a Nottinghamshire miner on the picket lines! ('yep that difficult')

As I've mentioned before the Toxteth and Brixton riots had sown the seeds for a lot of animosity between the black yoot and Joe Public, and with the Broadwater Farm riots fresh in the memory, we were walking targets for the police and establishment.

When we used to arrive at Turn Ups, my honky friends and I, I'd walk up the steps with the lads only to be stopped at the top while another bouncer went inside to check how many brothers were already inside. My friends would always wait in the foyer for me, and if I got the green light a huge cheer would go up as I waltzed in, paid the fee, then joined them in destroying the dance floor with what we thought at the time, revolutionary dance moves. On other occasions I'd lose my temper, tell the lads to enjoy the night, then tell the steroid pumped C**ts to f**k off, then head off home. There was only so much I was willing to take, and those nights tipped me over the edge.

One night I climbed the steps to Turn Ups when monkey man halted my progress while his sidekick stuck his head round the door. On his return it was a shake of the head and a "not tonight son", wankers, I'd had enough. I stormed down the stairs and went up town for some grub, when I walked past the club on my way home, monkey man called out "are you coming in or what?"

I stuffed down the Wimpey and fries in record time and walked in, the lads were pleased but surprised to see me because I'd told them to enjoy themselves and called it a (bad) night.

The late evening was going well, the disco lights were bright, the tunes were pumping, and I had chronic indigestion, I needed a drink. I went over to the bar, and out of the corner of my eye there she was, the lady in white, she looked like she was staring straight through me, maybe I wasn't the only looker in the place! So I turned round to confront the other handsome devil but there was no one there, hello I thought, we're in business.

It just so happens that my mate's mum and dad had just left that very morning for the Costa del no Rain, so he said we could all crash at his, and if we happened to hit the jackpot, our companions for the evening were also welcome. So I chatted with the lady in white for the remainder of the evening, asking her the usual ground breaking question "do you come here often" oh come on be fair, I was learning my craft. She was from Shiregreen, very well heeled compared to my home from home, but still proud all the same. I just couldn't take my eyes off her, even the ones in the back of my head shuffled round to see what the fuss was all about. We danced to a number of slow ballads such as Phyllis Nelson's 'Move Closer' and the song that became our standard, Kool and the Gang's 'Cherish'.

At the end of the night I then asked her if she wanted to come back to mateys for a while, and to my astonishment she said "yes ok". I was waiting for the sure fire knock back, but the boy done good result, this meant I would have to do things in style and pay the taxi driver what he was due, there was no chance of doing a runner tonight judging by my pull's white stilettos.

Paying the taxi driver felt good, this could turn out to be a regular thing. So we arrived at my mate's house but there were no lights on and not a sign of anyone around, so we waited for half an hour. That half an hour turned into two, we were freezing, the lady in white was turning blue, so I offered her my prized aqua blue Kappa jumper. She took it from me and smothered herself in it, now I was changing colour, I spotted a bedroom window open and thought I could get through it, I could let myself in and we could wait in the warmth.

I was about to squeeze through, when a thought just crept over me a young black yoot trying to force himself through an open window in the early hours of a Sunday morning would have alerted all the police stations in the surrounding areas with the good news. They'd have all scrambled to get here to make that all important bust, and that weekend in Paris for two.

We spent the whole night on the step, I was freezing, she was as warm as toast, she had my Chinos on.

After our romantic night underneath the stars, we walked down Manor Lane

97

and Granville and made our way to the Pond Street transport café. I must have downed five or six steaming hot mugs as we waited for her first bus home, the number 48 to pull out.

When she got on the bus she handed me half a beer mat with her number in eyeliner smudged on it, "call me" she said and then the bus pulled out.

Feeling really pleased with myself I walked through Park Hill and up Duke Street, but felt a little naked, then I realised the lady in white had made off with my Kappa;, shit! I was now betting the number on the ripped beer mat was indeed a false one.

Needless to say I saw my Kappa again, and her into the bargain. We used to meet in Paradise Square then stroll through the town 'til it was time for her to go home, I didn't know it then, but I'd just landed myself a first girlfriend of whom I used to think about day and night.

Turf war, and no matter what anyone says, two up against one just isn't fair, it just wasn't cricket old boy as our posh friends would say.

But that's the situation we found ourselves in as word had gotten out that two of Sheffield's most unlikeliest of allies had teamed up to (how can I put this) smash our faces in. I don't think anyone to this day knows why we found ourselves in the Rorke's Drift situation, but it was going to be a real test of one's character that's for sure. In turn we asked one of the Park Hill boys who was seeing a Wybourn lass at the time for help, he promised us he'd deliver with a tasty mob to join forces with us.

On the night of the showdown we all gathered on the Windsor wall with no ideas or plan of attack, in truth we were all over the place. To add to the chaos on the night, the Park Hill gang were a no show, they'd called in sick, probably from the warmth and comfort of the Scottish Queen with the curtains shut.

Anyway I had my own mini dilemma to deal with, because our aggressors were Darnall and Pitsmoor. How would I feel about planting one on the chin of what might have been most of my friends from school, who for most were from Darnall and the 'Cliffe?

Or how would I feel about knocking a brother out, my people from the other side of town?

Well the answer to those questions was no problems whatsoever, they were coming to hurt us, invading our land and they had to be stopped by any means necessary. Besides I wasn't a fighter more of a peacemaker if truth be told, I'd never had a fight (a real one) or thrown a punch in anger before but in defence of our estate I didn't have any problems.

Just so long as the bastards stayed away from the face and didn't touch the hair, we were in business.

There then followed a mad scramble to collect as many milk bottles as we could, and let me tell you there were hundreds all over the Windsor courtyard. The plan was to cover all the bases, we had no idea which way the invaders would come so we got hold of the old blue milk crates and took them full of bottles up to the cemetery gates, the alley that led onto Sky Edge and the black railings at the side of St Oswalds school.

Each potential entry point had foot soldiers patrolling waiting for the onslaught. The idea was to shower Darnall and Pitsmoor with as much glass as we could until the others joined us, it sounds rather barbaric, but compared to what the kids can do today, they were getting it easy.

There were a lot of nerves in the camp that night as we waited and waited but nothing, not even a single stranger to contend with. In the end we called of the high alert and started to do the things we normally did of an evening, sit on the wall laugh and joke and for some, skin up.

What! Oh the milk bottles, well we disposed of them on someone else's doorstep, I would have loved to have seen the milkman's face when he went through the gate whistling his merry tune, Gold top in hand, only to be confronted by 824 empties (I counted them).

My musical tastes were changing again once more, for better, for worse, I'll let you decide because I was now a massive fan of those Manchester poet songsters, The Smiths.

I'd borrowed their 'Queen is Dead' and 'Meat is Murder' tapes from a lad who used to hang with us off Sky Edge, Chris Lambing. I was blown away by the lyrics and the content of each song, the Smiths were no strangers to me, I'd heard their stuff before mainly the singles. My first introduction to the band was a Top Of The Pops performance where I can vividly remember asking a friend at school "did you see that tosser with the flowers sprouting from his back pocket?"

Staying on the music front, me and a pal devised a way of making some quick and easy money, it was fool proof.

We decided to buy the latest albums or cassettes of the most popular groups of the day, tape them, and then take back the records or cassettes to the shop of which they came.

Backed by a stack of TDK blank tapes, we took orders from the top middle and bottom end of the Wybourn estate. The most popular one we did was Tears for Fears 'Songs From The Big Chair' (an excellent choice madam.)

What with my business patter and smooth talking and his Err! Err! We were raking in a fair bit of loose change (club money) and put some of it back into the enterprise. We ripped off all the record shops in and around Sheffield. All except for one, and that was Roulette Records on the High Street.

Roulette was run by big Kev who's girlfriend just happened to be Tony and Dinky Dawson's sister Ann, and you know what they say never shit on your own doorstep, and more importantly, never shaft your own.

Everything was going great until buddy boy lost his bottle and decided to dissolve the partnership, so I decided to go it alone. But there's only so much one fat cat can do himself and the YEB were loving the new arrangement, because mum's bill was starting to hit the roof.

When the time came to meet my new girlfriend's parents arrived I was a nervous wreck, we both were, it was 1985 and mixed race relationships were still being frowned upon. Not like it is today, they were as common as owning a mobile phone back then but if you love someone..!

Teen Daddy...

"'Oh no it's the law again". I'd just come out of Atkinson's on the Moor, when I felt a tap on my shoulder (hey mind the chip!) I turned round and there was PC stitch up smiling at me.

"Excuse me sir", did I hear that right did he just call me sir? I looked to my left, then to my right and then behind me, there was no one else there, damn that Jeremy Beadle's good.

The copper then asked me whether I'd be interested in taking part in an ID parade down at West Bar, all voluntary like, and for forty to sixty minutes of my time a fee of fifteen quid cash would be paid. Right there and then I had a hunch the suspect wasn't white (would have made a great detective me!) so I thought why not and asked for more details.

The copper said he'd explain on the way down to the station and directed me to a waiting Z car, but I refused point blank to get in it insisting instead of making my own way there. Can you imagine what people would have been thinking seeing me on a busy shopping day being escorted into a police car. I really hate it when people put two and two together and get four.

So when I hit the station, I was taken up to the office where the ID parade would take place. It was a bit of a shock seeing all the other suspects because they looked like real down and outs, was that copper trying to tell me something.

I hope not, not with a Lacoste polo and cardy combo, Wrangler cords and a brand new, just out of the box, pair of Gazelles on my feet - cheeky twat.

The really unsettling thing about the ID parade is that one of us was as guilty as sin, but who?

I had no idea what the frame up was, but when we were asked to stand up and face the front another copper brought in a young white female. She looked as though she'd just been in an almighty scrap with Frank Bruno (not a mark on her see) she studied each of our faces with intensity. She was really pretty too, there might even have been a date in the offing after all this.

As she walked the line she stopped at me and another suspect a real shady character, "that's your man I thought", she started to study us long and hard making me feel really uncomfortable. She started to make me feel rather nervous, it wasn't funny anymore, "come out Jeremy you bastard".

What I really wanted to do was shout out I was a volunteer, but that was out of the question, so I carried on sweating for what seemed like hours.

When the parade was over I was shaking like a leaf, the copper reassured me I had nothing to worry about, but just in case where was I on the night of the 12th between 10pm and 12?

When the day did arrive for me to meet my new girlfriend's parents my heart was beating so fast and loud, you could hear it a mile away. Her dad was a striking miner and good for him, don't let the bastards turn you over son. The atmosphere wasn't a happy one, but they had each other, and I admired that - one out, all out. When I walked in, dad was reading the Star newspaper, and if you can remember, the Star used to stand so high, so it would cover the top half of your body as you read.

He said hello from behind the paper, and then we went upstairs to play the latest Bronski Beat tunes, or something like that. When it was time to leave, I said my goodbyes with dad still hid behind the paper.

This went on for a couple of days, hello and goodbye from behind the paper. I'd like to think he already knew I was of the black persuasion before his baby grandson was dumped on his lap. Her parents used to go out to the local social club, The Bellhouse I think it was. That left us alone in the house to do anything we wanted to do, or so we thought.

My girlfriend had a little sister who used to sit between us all the time and wouldn't budge unless the price was right. I used to go across to the shop and come back with a stack of pop, crisps, chocolate and sweets and that would do the job for a while. But only until she'd gone through the lot in her bedroom, then she'd be back sat slap bang in the middle of us again. One day I reached out for the Yellow Pages and looked under hit men for hire, but they tended to shy away from that sort of thing. I tried everything to capture a precious moment with my woman but it just wasn't happening. So it was time for some pest control, it was time to put plan W into action.

Little sister was a huge fan of Madonna at the time, after the American singer had burst onto the scene the year before, and she couldn't get enough.

So with that vital piece of info in my locker, I made a beeline for Woolworths in town, and headed straight for the record department. Madonna had just released her new single, 'Angel', and I snapped up a copy with a huge grin all over my face because the year before Madonna had sung about being a virgin, now here she was helping me with mine, the Big V.

That evening we were all squashed up on the sofa all three of us when I pulled it out (the record silly), her sisters eyes lit up (the record silly). She leapt up from the sofa and disappeared for the rest of the evening. It was as easy as that, we'd wasted all that time on Abracadabra.

I got myself a full time job, building and erecting sheds. My duties were going out with the drivers all over the north and putting these sheds together. Most of the business was in Manchester in the heart of the Jewish community. And on top of my wages of sixty-five pounds per week, there were generous tips of which I'd spend on my girl.

If I stayed in the yard I'd paint or dye the sheds that had just been put together and along with general dogs body duties, life was ok. Legend has it my boss was less than squeaky clean on the side, and the taxman wasn't top of his Christmas card list. I started checking my wages, especially the notes very carefully under the light bulb.

It didn't take long for my friends to suss out where I was disappearing to in the evenings, it all came about when one of the lads had moved up to Shiregreen with his parents, and it was there I was spotted by rest of the gang who used to visit him. Very soon they'd all be joining me having met other girls on the estate, which didn't please the local boys one little bit. We were modern day vikings, running amok on someone else's turf, take, take, take, and giving nothing back.

On a good day we'd all pile onto the number 47 or 48 whichever came first, get off at the green, then all go our separate ways on the estate loving all the girls. I made a lot of friends on the green, more than I could ever have imagined, everyone knew my girlfriend and her family, they were a really popular bunch. I befriended two prostitutes who used to catch the same bus every evening with me, and got to know them really well. I tried to understand why they did what they did, and to a certain extent I did understand. After all with the onset of high unemployment and Norman Tebbit's infamous get on your bikes speech these two lovely girls decided to become the two wheeled run around instead. When my girl went over to Germany, where the kids of striking miners were given a free holiday courtesy of the miners welfare, I missed her like I've never missed anyone in my life.

The fortnight she was away nearly destroyed me, I hated Arthur Scargill every moment she was away. I was head over heels with her and if I didn't know it before, I had it rubber stamped for me during the time we had apart.

On my 18th birthday, there were no party poppers, streamers or a huge cake to celebrate the milestone, far from it, no on my 18th birthday I was pacing frantically up and down on the maternity wing of the Northern General Hospital, an expectant father to be. Suddenly that Madonna single had a lot to answer for, it only seemed like yesterday that my own mum had walked out of the joint with me the newest member of our family tree, I bet her bed was still warm.

My girlfriend had dropped the bombshell, oh let me see, yeah nine months before she gave birth, I can remember nearly feeling sick at the prospect. Not because I couldn't handle it, but because of what my mother would say. For me I couldn't get my head round the fact that this kid was having a kid, a little life to look and watch over for the rest of my life.

I have to say mum was fantastic about the whole affair, I think she knew deep down that all that shouting and disappointment raised couldn't reverse the fact that she was to become a nan. My girlfriend's parents were equally supportive, and I even caught a glimpse of grandad to be's face *(The Star* wasn't printed on a Sunday').

It was to be an experience I wouldn't ever forget because baby didn't want to set foot outside its comfort zone when the time came to vacate the womb, it was a difficult birth. In the end the doctors had to use forceps to pull out the newest member of the clan, I couldn't watch I almost fell apart.

Our relationship continued but under difficult circumstances, I used to go up to Shiregreen everyday to see the two most important people in my life, but things were changing fast.

My girlfriend and our baby son were living with her parents and sister in very cramped conditions, and to give her a break from motherhood, I used to take my son home with me to see my mum, sister and the full guided tour of the Wybourn estate.

But for all the help I tried to provide the cracks were starting to appear, we were drifting apart and it was breaking my heart, and to add insult to injury there was someone else waiting in the wings to take my place.

We'd argue at full throttle on a daily basis about this and about that, and I'd become insanely jealous of anyone other than myself who talked to her or approached her. I was slowly losing my grip on the woman I loved and reality.

When the day of the break up came I didn't ever envisage never seeing my son again, I never saw it coming. I really thought that we'd remain friends for life and that time would heal the rift that had eaten away at our love for each other. But sinister forces were at work driving a huge wedge between any chances of reconciliation, and an end to the bitter rift that had taken a hold of us.

My rival was like a circling vulture waiting for the remainder of our love to die, and when it finally did he'd be there to pick at the remaining remnants on the carcass of love and life.

There was a happy ending though, because at the age of eighteen my son found me, and in turn I introduced him to his long lost family. All he ever knew was his white mother, white step father, white brothers and grandparents, so as we all hugged in my mother's small kitchen with tears welling up in our eyes, I had one solitary thought., "welcome to the dark side son, welcome to the dark side". Oh and just for the record, I have no lingering bitterness toward my first girlfriend, nor do I bare any grudges. A lot of water has flowed under the bridge since then, and I wish her all the best in life. For twenty six years I've never laid eyes on her, and if she were to lap dance in my face, I don't think I'd recognise her now, but I just want you to know one thing.

God forbid, but if you should ever find yourself engulfed in flames, I would gladly piss on you to put you out, my lady in white.

At home, new neighbours meant new kids on the block, so joining the seasoned pro's in the keyhole were, Patricia, Kathleen, Edward, Lee, Tracey, Lindsey and last but not least our new next door neighbours the Brady Bunch.

After the upheaval of losing my woman, I'd knocked the clubbing scene on the head for a while, I was hurt, I was wounded my pride had taken a huge kick in the gonads, and it would take a little time to recover.

It never rains it just pours, the dark clouds were up above and things got even worse for me when I was laid off at work. It was the old last one in first one out bullshit, so feeling sorry for myself I fled to the comfort of my bedroom and shut the door on the world outside. The nights out were over, a thing of the past as I spiralled into a reclusive world of my own making. I used to watch my good mates file in to the Windsor on a Friday and Saturday night, then watch as they either boarded the 56 bus into town, or if they were feeling really flush a (DB) taxi. Suited and booted I let them leave the estate without me, I wanted out I was no longer the same fun loving kid I used to be. Most of my time was spent listening to the radio, listening out for the next big thing, and one evening on a Bruno Brookes show I received exactly what I had tuned in for.

The band was from Glasgow and had just released their debut album 'Raintown', and on the night in question they had performed a couple of tracks from the album in a live session for Bruno. Deacon Blue blew me away, it was new, it was exciting and it was just what the end of the decade needed, freshness. Along with the session Bruno also championed the new Prince album Sign o the times which also captivated me, soon after that those two albums were sitting on my record shelf.

I joined another YTS type scheme at this point, you were allowed to do one more back in the day and this one was centred around the 18 to 21s.

The work we did varied, you could almost do anything you wanted to do from dry stone walling to farming.

I decided to do the decorating thing again and was assigned to go up to Hope Valley to help give a big stately home a lick of paint and a much needed colour makeover.

The house was huge and it held court to many a visitor who would come for breaks out in the country, it also hosted school parties with rock climbing, pony trekking and a host of other outdoor activities. I used to travel up there with the gardening team who would tend to the grounds and the upkeep of the surrounding areas on the estate. I teamed up with another lad from Shiregreen who became a really good friend and the two of us would spruce up the place with the radio blasting out ska, mod, motown, northern soul, and the usual '80s pop. Sometimes we didn't want to stop working, we were having such a great time of it, and along with getting the work done we were also having a lorra lorra laughs.

The National Trust organisation sponsored the whole thing and I loved every minute of my time there, I slowly learnt how to be a young youth again.

In the mornings we'd be picked up outside the Saddle pub, then we'd make our way to Hillsborough Corner then turn left through Rivelin bound for Hope Valley. Once we got there me and the other decorator would go off to do the Rolf Harris bit, while the rest of the crew the gardeners would do there bit in an around the grounds of the stately home.

At dinner times we'd all meet up in the small wooden cabin for lunch, then we'd play cricket on the lush green grass that had just been freshly mown.

I became close friends with another lad off the gardening team who was bit of a hard nut, nothing phased him he was a real gung ho kind of kid, always knocking people out.

But underneath all the macho, Rambo bravado was a true friend, someone who you could rely on in the trenches when the bullets were flying in all directions.

I'd decided not to trust another woman again, love stinks was my new philosophy and manifesto, but all that changed when one of the lads had told me that I had gained an admirer, someone who worked in the clerical department at head office.

Now the only time we ventured up to the head office was on Fridays to collect our wages which was paid out in cash, so there hardly seemed enough time for someone to have a crush on me, but I was interested to know who all the same. The bird in question was from up Dore/Totley and my first thought was what would she want with a Wybourn low life like me? Was she getting back at her parents for something or what?

Turns out she was a really nice girl and I was immediately attracted to her, but the demons were telling me to do a runner, not to get involved or sucked in again.

We got on handsomely and the inevitable date was on the horizon. She made me laugh with her plum in the gob accent and her whole outlook on life, she was an only child and spoiled something rotten. Holidays abroad, sking trips and pocket money that would have made a premiership footballer blush. Her parents were, and still are, fine upstanding people; dad was big in education with the power to hire and fire teachers at his will, or close down schools or save them depending on what mood he was in.

If only I had have met his daughter when I was twelve, I could have wiped out Waltheof Comprehensive with one simple phone call! Mum was a retired teacher and an avid Christian scientist... Yeah me neither! But they welcomed me into the fold with open arms.

You wouldn't find the *Sun* newspaper in this household, no chance, it was the *Guardian, Horse and Hound* and *Cosmopolitan* for coffee time reading. In fact the one time I did bring the Sun newspaper into their home it was met with a double barrelled tut tut from ma and pa.

We went on a string of dates, and some of the places we went wouldn't have even been considered on our booze cruise (the lads) Henry's Mr Kites very la di da, but she loved it then we'd end up at Isabella's for the rest of the night.

When we weren't out we'd spend time in her bedroom watching our favourite American sitcom which was old re runs of the odd couple (very apt) starring Tony Randall and Jack Klugman (that's *Quincy* to you and me!)

I spent most of my time with her and went home only to change my clothes and collect any post, I was gradually moving out. From Wybourn to Totley, now that's what I call one giant leap for mankind Mr Neil Armstrong me old china.

I went back to Granville to do a GCSE course in history and English literature and gained two Bs, I was also becoming well read in history, politics and the arts.

I could also hold my own round my new girlfriend's parents' dinner table, I gave her mum what for when she gave the Iron Lady the big thumbs at Number Ten.

Having ignored my demons and put them in their place, everything was rosy but, and there's always a but (I'm sure I've said that before!), the dark clouds were gathering to shower me with more heartache and grief by the bucket load.

All Roads Lead To... Roxy's

Aciieed, aciieed, aciieed. My beloved '80s was on the verge of being just another decadent decade, as acid house reigned supreme and the Manchester mafia were planning a takeover of the early '90s.

So here I was, I'd gone from the lady in white to Lady Penelope Pitstop in the space of fourteen months, and with it a change in appearance a makeover. I felt on top of the world. My afro had vanished completely whilst still with the lady in white preferring to have my hair relaxed, or if you're from across the water in the States, a jerry curl.

I went up London Road and headed toward Palm Court, a hairdresser that specialised in Afro Caribbean hair. My head was full of chemicals during the process and my eyes and ears were on fire.

After the experts washed all the gunk out of my hair my head felt a couple of pounds lighter, but I loved the end result. With swept back hair, designer stubble and Top Shop's summer collection hanging from my rails, I was starting to resemble a black Sonny Crockett.

My mates were only catching glimpses of me now, the love bug had bitten again, and the love of a good woman was more than they had to offer as a collective.

Then just when I thought it was safe to dip my toes back in the water, ouch, Penelope announced she was pregnant.

The moment she told me I became a member of the white human race as the colour drained away from my face with the life changing news, part 2.

As parents do, her mum and dad were worried for their only daughter's wellbeing and discussed all the options such as getting a place of our own, or living with the future in laws until we felt we were ready to go it alone.

Whatever Penelope wanted, I was one hundred percent behind her, I loved her and would have done anything to make her happy. So much for love stinks eh, the manifesto was ripped into a million tiny pieces. Our baby daughter was born in the summer of '89, and after a brief stint living with Penelope's parents we got ourselves a flat on the Norfolk Park Estate.

Now I had nothing but admiration for Penelope at this point because this was my neck of the woods, for her it was a different world all together, a very different world indeed.

At weekends she would go home to her parent's house and spend the weekends in the splendour she was accustomed to, and who could blame her? When I used to leave the flat she'd bolt the door shut, she didn't know anyone and her new surroundings were alien like, I did feel for her because she'd never seen anything like it before.

There were neighbours' throwing rubbish, nappies etc, etc from up above onto the ground below, graffiti everywhere, and don't even get me started on the lifts.

It was all water off a ducks back for me, but for her it was water off a ducks back mixed in with oil from a stricken fuel tanker.

I worked abroad during her pregnancy, London, (well it was abroad for me having never been before), I hated the place but I was bringing home top money, so I had to grin and bare it.

There was no way I could do the same thing now, she was frightened and didn't want to be alone.

I wanted to do what was best for Penelope and our child, but I was losing the battle to keep her.

The final straw came when we were turned over, and the television and video were stolen, I think she came home to find the door off its hinges. Right there and then I knew I had to let her go, it just wasn't fair anymore. She'd had enough plus my constant mood swings didn't help matters much either.

When the day came for her to move out it hit me hard, I didn't want her to leave but I had nothing left to give, I couldn't guarantee a life of suburban happiness. This resulted in me having a massive breakdown, I was on the edge of insanity, I wanted Penelope back but was going about it the wrong way, making me one of the most despised people on the planet. My depression hit an all time low when I just let myself go. My appearance was shot and my mind was wandering into some really dark places. And believe me eight floors up in a tower block listening to the Smiths and Morrissey doesn't really bode well for the future.

The flat became my prison, I could venture out whenever I pleased but all I could see before me were bars. Things really took a turn for the worse when I walked up to Totley in the rain and pitch darkness. I was half naked with no shoes or trainers on my feet to plead with Penelope to come home. I was in a daze and just walked with no sense of direction. I was close to the edge, too close and it took a visit from two special people to help me realise that people did care for me, and loved me, and didn't want to see me slip away.

My mum and my sister paid a visit one evening but I didn't open the door to them, I guess they knew I was home though because they were talking through the letterbox. Words of encouragement filled the flat, while I sat on the floor with tears streaming down my face.

When they left I crept up to the window and watched them walk off into the distance having tried so desperately to lure me out.

My best friend didn't pull any punches either, I towered over him but he didn't let that little detail stop him from booting me up the arse and slapping me around in a vain attempt at smartening me up. It was time to stop feeling sorry for myself and get back to being the streetwise kid everyone knew and hopefully loved.

The road to recovery was helped greatly by seeing my daughter anytime I wanted, within reason of course. My relationship with Penelope was steady, we never argued just disagreed on certain subjects. When she informed me of her new relationship with another man, I shocked her and myself by giving her my blessing. Not that she needed it, but the most important thing for me was her and my daughter's happiness, and he sounded like a really nice guy too.

She obviously made the right choice as they became man and wife, and still remain as strong as ever to this very day, I've met him on numerous occasions and I have to say he really is a splendid fellow indeed.

Picking up the pieces from another broken relationship wasn't going to be easy, my self confidence and worth were in tatters.

But you know me, I'll try anything once (or twice).

And so my friends this is where we part company, a quarter of a century in.

But don't worry because I'll be back (yeah, thanks Arnie!) bigger, better and bolder than ever before, trust me.

Now all you have to do is to remember to fasten your seat belts tightly for the next 25 year instalment.

So until then good luck, god bless and take good care of yourselves.

Oh just one more thing before I go.

I tried my best to avoid one of those really annoying clichés to round things off, you know the one: "You can take the boy out of the Wybourn, but you can't take the Wybourn out of the boy."

Last word:

Special thank yous and a huge shake of the hand to...

Beryl and George aka Mummy and Daddy. Thanks for life.

My sister Tracey (I think I can do better than a handshake) a massive brother hug. Thanks for sharing that life, the early years.

My children, a second generation born to these shores. You are a very rich source of inspiration to me, I love you.

My niece Natasha, thanks for the help with the 21st century side of things and the countless hours typing your fingers to the bone.

My partner Jenine, for loving this rough around the edges Wybourn lad, council fodder as I'm affectionately known indoors. I wouldn't mind but she's only off the Hackers.

A very big shout out to my extended family, that's you the men, women, boys and girls past and present who have trod the promised land.

A very special mention for the Wybourn friends we lost along the way (R.I.P.) never forgotten.

The Specials who single handedly saved 1979.

Thelma and Ron.

Mr Neil Anderson, a modern day captain of industry and the staff of ACM Retro (nice one).

Sheffield Newspapers for use of the photos.

And finally Kath I'm sorry, I'm older, I'm wiser and full of remorse.

Also available from  www.acmretro.com

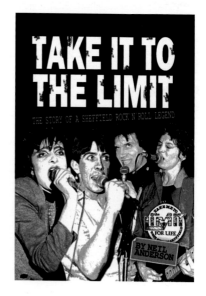